Essex
MURDERS

Linda Stratmann

Sutton Publishing

First published in the United Kingdom in 2004 by
Sutton Publishing Limited · Phoenix Mill
Thrupp · Stroud · Gloucestershire · GL5 2BU

Copyright © Linda Stratmann, 2004

Series Consulting Editor: Stewart P. Evans

British Library Cataloguing in Publication Data
A catalogue record for this book is available from the British Library.

ISBN 0-7509-3554-5

To John,
Essex boy extraordinaire

Typeset in 10.5/13.5pt Sabon
Typesetting and origination by
Sutton Publishing Limited.
Printed and bound in England by
J.H. Haynes & Co. Ltd, Sparkford.

CONTENTS

INTRODUCTION

Each of these ten tales of murder in Essex reveals something of the rich history of the county, and the variety of its landscape. Salt-marshes, a doomed airfield, a protected forest, cornfields dotted with windmills, sandy beaches, industrial townships, country manors and lonely roads may all provide the backdrop to murder. Some of these stories are being anthologised for the first time, and I make no apologies for omitting the better-known and often-told tales in favour of the freshness of these new classics. We all love a good story, and for drama, the human touch and the occasional dizzying twist, these are unbeatable. And they are all true.

I have used only contemporary documents as my sources – accounts of inquests and trials which were fully reported in pamphlets and newspapers of the day, the memoirs of Superintendent Totterdell who personally investigated three of the cases, and documents held in local study archives, the Essex Police Museum, the Family Record Centre, the Essex County Archives, and the United States Army Judiciary.

1
COLCHESTER JACK, 1744–6

S mugglers have usually enjoyed a romantic reputation, and few more so than John Skinner. Well-known among his fraternity in Boulogne as Saucy Jack or Colchester Jack, he was the Casanova of smugglers. Handsome, and well dressed, he no doubt had manners which women found attractive, for he was adept at enticing married ladies from their husbands, and deluding single women that they were the sole object of his attentions.

He was born in Brightlingsea, in 1704, the son of John and Mary Skinner, sound middle-class folk, who did everything good parents should have done to teach him that advancement should come through honesty and hard work. He was provided with a good education, and in due course was apprenticed to a respectable and well-established wholesale dealer in oil, whose place of business was near St Andrew's Church, Holborn, London. If his parents had a fault it was in over-indulging their son, so that as he left childhood and entered his wilder years, he continued to believe that he could have anything he wanted – and what he wanted he took. When thwarted of his desires, he would burst into a rage at those who opposed him. Predictably, his apprenticeship did not go smoothly, for he took liberties not appropriate to his humble position, but somehow all his little flights of folly were passed over as youthful high sprits. When the period of his apprenticeship was over, his proud parents set him up in business in a neat and well-furnished shop just outside Aldgate.

John Skinner was on his way to being a prosperous man. He married an attractive young woman from a good Essex family who brought with her a fortune of some £5,000 (about £475,000 today). The connections of both his own and his wife's families brought a great deal of business his way, and before long he was supplying the greater part of the county.

Money rolled in, but John Skinner believed that there was only one thing to do with money, and that was to spend it on his own personal pleasures. His three weaknesses were, predictably, drink, gambling and women, and he took to spending much of his time in brothels, neglecting both his wife and his business. On one occasion he was heard to declare that he had been at a bawdy-house for ten days successively during which time he had spent £60 to £70.

If he had considered his business at all, he must have thought that his servants would take care of it, but they soon took advantage of his frequent absences and made away with both his money and his goods. Skinner, more than other men, must have known that servants may be tempted by the

Brightlingsea parish church, where John Skinner was baptised and buried. (Author's Collection)

indolence of their master, but when he sobered up enough to have a look at his books, he was very surprised to find a substantial deficiency. While complaining bitterly about the situation, he was too far gone in his life of debauchery and profligate spending to mend his ways.

His wife, powerless to do anything to improve the situation, and seeing her fortune being slowly consumed, hardly knew which way to turn. She may have felt ashamed of her position, or believed that it was something she should be able to deal with herself – at any rate she was not able to bring herself to tell her parents what was happening. She was a woman of good education, knowledgeable about her husband's business, well-mannered and patient. When he was home she tried to advise him as best she could, but, as a contemporary observed 'he was one of those fine Gentlemen that could not bear to be talk'd to by a Woman'.

Skinner liked to live well, kept a brace of fine geldings and liveried servants, but when out and about taking his pleasures, seldom included his wife in the party, 'some demolish'd Beau, Gamester, Sharper, . . . or Bawdy-house Keeper, were his constant companions; and he was so well known amongst those gentry, that he got the Name of Squire Skinner'.

This situation could not go on indefinitely, and in a few years the inevitable happened, and Skinner found himself unable to pay his debts. A bankruptcy order was taken out against him, and it was found that he owed in total £10,000, though when the commission was finally closed he was able to pay his creditors 15s in the pound.

Having settled that little matter Skinner thought no more of the oil business, and indeed no more of his wife, who was brought to a state of utter destitution and was obliged to enter the parish workhouse. Though Skinner was to prosper in the future he was never to send his wife a single shilling for her support. He left London, and returned to his roots in Essex, where he took an inn at Romford, called the King's Head. It was here he discovered that large profits could be obtained with very little work in the business of smuggling, and was immediately attracted to a way of life that seemed to be ideal for his tastes. Before long, he was one of the most notorious smugglers in the County of Essex.

Evading taxes has always been a popular pastime, and the imposition of high duties on desirable luxury goods will naturally attract the opportunist. In the eighteenth century, frequent wars prompted the government to raise finances by taxing imports such as Dutch gin, French brandy, tobacco and tea. At the same time, there were insufficient resources of men and ships to keep a watch on the coast. The result was a thriving industry of smuggling. The potential profits were high – in the 1740s the duty on tea was 4s per lb. Of the annual consumption of 1½ million lb duty was actually collected on only 650,000lb, a loss to the government of £170,000, (nearly £18 million today).

At first sight the coastline of Essex would seem to offer little opportunity to the smuggler. A large vessel, seeking to land its cargo would find few suitable places to approach undetected. Some of the rare locations that offered such easy access were Clacton, Frinton and Walton. There, landing contraband cargo from large ships would involve not just a few men but most of the local community. Labourers would assemble under cover of dark to help carry the goods, receiving payment in kind, and there was plenty of sparsely populated land where packages and barrels could be hidden, or moved without hindrance to a final destination in the larger towns, or even to London. Many publicans were actively involved in the trade, relying on cheap alcohol to stock their cellars, and there can have been few people of quality unaware of just how their silks and lace had arrived onshore.

Unfortunately for would-be smugglers, much of the Essex coastline is flat salt-marshes, with narrow inlets for shipping. Not only would a large vessel be too conspicuous in such a setting, its only means of approach to the inland harbours such as Colchester would place it in danger of having its escape route blocked. The alternative was for the laden ship to anchor out to sea at a safe distance, while the smugglers took small fishing boats out to collect the goods. They could then sail back between the sand banks where the larger Revenue ships could not follow, and land their cargo in the desolate marshlands between Wivenhoe and Brightlingsea.

Those few officials appointed to guard the coast were, for the most part, courageous and conscientious men, who were nevertheless overwhelmed by the enormity of the task, and often quite rightly hesitant to tackle gangs of armed criminals. In the early part of the eighteenth century there were, between Harwich and Colchester no customs officers at all, and just two boatmen at Brightlingsea. In 1721 matters were slightly improved by the appointment of an officer with an assistant, but there was a strong suspicion that the assistant was more than usually friendly with three of the most active smugglers in the area.

With most of the local community benefiting from the trade it was inevitable that smugglers felt they could rely on their fellow-townsfolk of every rank of society not to reveal their hiding places or movements. Even if prosecuted, the justices were reluctant to lose a source of discount luxuries. In 1731 at the Chelmsford Assizes a known villain, John Lilley, was tried for obstructing customs officers, and, much to their disgust, the judge ordered his acquittal without allowing the prosecution evidence to be given.

Local popularity gave smugglers their reputation as dashing fellows, but many were hardened and brutal men, carrying weapons, and not averse to committing murder. Such was the reputation of smugglers for callous violence that in 1736 an Act of Parliament was passed imposing the death penalty on smugglers who used arms against customs officials. Resisting arrest even if unarmed carried the penalty of flogging, transportation or imprisonment with hard labour. While this may seem severe, the actuality was that lesser penalties were often imposed instead, such as seizure of goods – a popular measure with the Customs official – or condemning the smuggler's vessel. It was rarely felt to be worthwhile to prosecute a minor offender.

No one knows exactly how John Skinner operated his smuggling business. Did he roughen his hands on a fishing boat, putting to sea to collect packages of contraband, or was he a land-dwelling 'Mr Big' who financed the operation and relied on paid assistants to do the hard work? One known associate was Daniel Brett, often described as a servant to Skinner but also very much his partner in the smuggling enterprises.

Skinner soon abandoned the Inn at Romford, and moved to Colchester, where he was known to keep company with men and women of bad character. While his main business was now smuggling he sought to disguise this by renting two farms, called the Tan-Office and Cox's Farm, each at £20 per annum, at Old Heath in the Parish of St Giles, and it was in a house on this heath that he was living in 1744. Elizabeth Cooper, a single lady, resided there as his housekeeper.

At 8 p.m. on the evening of 23 May, Skinner arrived home to keep an appointment. He had sent for a tailor called John Rallett also of St Giles,

Colchester, to do some business with him. In his later statement, Rallett did not reveal quite what this business was except that it was connected with tailoring, and he left it to the courts to assume that what Skinner had been after was a suit of clothes. Since Skinner was known to deal in smuggled lace, it may well have been that the true nature of Rallett's business was to purchase some contraband goods. When Skinner arrived, Miss Cooper at once drew him aside and had a conversation with him in a low tone of voice, which Rallett could not properly hear, but he gained the impression she was referring to a person and also some things, which were in a place he could not hear named. According to Miss Cooper's statement, she was informing Skinner that some of the goods he had stored in the house were missing. It seemed that Daniel Brett, his partner-in-crime, had arrived there earlier and taken away some packages which the two men had smuggled together. Skinner at once flew into a violent temper, 'and said that he would have his goods again, for he had ventured his life for them once, and would venture his life again for them, for that he would either kill or be killed'. He demanded she fetch him his powder horn, which she did, and stated 'I will shoot him as dead as a carrion-crow, and then let him go and ask pardon of God Almighty'. Skinner loaded his carbine. He called for a dram of drink which she gave to him, and having swallowed it down, he left the house, and, with the words 'now for conquest, liberty or death!', mounted his horse, and rode away. If this was only to do with some missing goods, it does seem like something of an overreaction, but this explosion of temper was very much in keeping with his known character.

Contemporary print of Colchester in the eighteenth century. (The Modern Universal British Traveller)

Old Colchester town hall, demolished in 1893. (History and Description of the Ancient Town and Borough of Colchester, T.K. Cromwell, 1825)

It was then about 8.30 p.m., and Rallett departed. Miss Cooper waited some hours for her master's return, but eventually retired for the night.

Skinner was searching for Daniel Brett. At about 10 p.m. he arrived at the house of Thomas Page, a victualler, and asked for Brett. Page said that Brett wasn't there, and Skinner again started to rage, cursing bitterly, saying that wherever he found Brett he would shoot him dead that night.

At some later hour, Skinner did catch up with Brett, but when or where this was, and precisely what passed between them is not recorded. What cannot be doubted is that Skinner shot Brett as he had promised to do, and it seems probable that he then took the wounded man to his own house, for that is the next place he was reported to be.

It was at about midnight that Skinner returned home in a state of great agitation calling to Miss Cooper that she should get out of bed at once, and come to the window. She complied, and demanded that he tell her for God's sake what the matter was. He spoke in a great hurry and with some confusion, and was unable to make a coherent answer, then abruptly, he turned away from the house and rode back full speed to Colchester. Not knowing what could be the matter, but suspecting that she would get no more sleep that night, Miss Cooper lit a candle, went downstairs and tended the fire, so she could sit by it and await her master's return. She had not been sitting there long when Daniel Brett entered, his clothing heavily stained with blood. She saw that he was badly wounded through the body, and did what she could for him.

Skinner, having shot Brett as he had been threatening to do for some hours past was by now panicking at the result of his own actions. Between 12 and 1 p.m. he was back at Colchester and arrived at the house of Thomas Brand, a surgeon. Skinner at once called to him to get up as he needed his assistance as a man was shot, and feared he was dead or would die. He demanded that Brand go with him immediately. Brand quickly prepared to go with Skinner, but he had gained the distinct impression from Skinner's manner that it was he who had carried out the shooting. As he got himself ready he asked Skinner what Brett had been shot with and Skinner confirmed that he had shot Brett with his carbine. Despite this worrying development, Brand went with Skinner to his house and there found Daniel Brett, with a wound in his body. There was no real treatment he could offer, indeed his sole action seems to have been to probe and search the wound, finding the bowels of the ailing man much lacerated and torn. The wound was triangular in shape and about half an inch long and as much wide, but he thought it was about ten inches deep. Whether he gave any kind of pain relief to Brett, such as opium, or whether the unfortunate man was unconscious or conscious during this examination he didn't record. In the eighteenth century such a wound was almost inevitably fatal, and his probing can hardly have helped.

Brand returned home, but came back to see Brett the next morning at 9 a.m., when the suffering man was still alive. He lingered until 11 or 12 noon, and when Brand came back again that afternoon, he found his patient dead. Miss Cooper reported that several times she had asked him who gave him the wound, but he would never answer the question. If true, this is a remarkable piece of loyalty on Brett's part, but Miss Cooper may well have been putting in a little invention to help her master.

The news of the murder had already spread around the district. Clement Boreham, a butcher of East Denyland, called at Skinner's house between 2 or 3 p.m. and found Brett there dead, as reported. By now, it seems that Skinner was over his panic. Life, and trade, must go on. The fact that he had just murdered a man was not to hold up his normal business activities. That same day, Boreham heard that Skinner had some pigs and cows to sell, and went in search of him to buy the goods. Skinner was out and about in a place called Denyland Heath, about a mile from where he had shot Brett. Skinner told Boreham that he had found Brett in company with four or five people conveying away goods – almost certainly smuggled merchandise – in bags and sacks.

According to Boreham, he and Skinner then talked about the pigs and cows. A Mrs Bevan who was present, was more forthright and asked Skinner how he could be so passionate to shoot the poor man, to which Skinner replied, 'I wish I had been in heaven; I am an unfortunate man, and wish I had never done it.'

Matters moved slowly. There is no record of Skinner being officially questioned about Brett's fate, but on 26 May, the various witnesses to the events of the fatal night were gathered together and examined separately and each gave their own story, swearing an affidavit.

It must have dawned upon Skinner eventually that if he remained in the neighbourhood he would soon be under arrest. Justice had paused too long, and when it came looking for him, John Skinner was nowhere to be found. It is assumed that he left the area and lived incognito for a while. Had he continued to do so, he might never have been caught. In the interim, the matter was brought before the courts, and a Bill of Indictment was found by the Grand Inquest against John Skinner for the wilful murder of Daniel Brett, but where the murderer was, no one seemed to know.

Nearly two years later, Skinner came into some property, and he must have had friends who secretly advised him of his good fortune. It wasn't especially valuable, an estate worth just £15 per annum (about £1,500 today), and the snag, from the point of view of a man in hiding, was that in order to claim the property, he was required to attend a copyhold court in person to effect the transfer. A sensible man might have decided to let it go. John Skinner was not that man. Assuming perhaps that his past indiscretions had been forgotten he strolled into the court on 29 April 1746 with as much assurance as if he was not guilty of any crime at all, and apparently without any fear that he might be brought to justice. He was recognised at once, and Mr Grayes the steward of the court being informed of the Bill of Indictment, at once had him arrested and committed to the County Gaol in Chelmsford.

Whatever Skinner had been doing since the murder, it had been profitable, for on being confined to gaol it was found that he had plenty of money and could therefore be indulged with every comfort he required, as far as was consistent with security. He was carefully watched, as it was thought that he would try to escape, but he never seemed inclined to make the attempt. He appeared perfectly confident that he would be acquitted, an opinion which no one else felt able to share with him. Skinner was very active in promoting his version of the events of 23 May 1744, which was that he had shot Brett while his associate had been attempting to rob him, but there was too much knowledge of the man and his methods for anyone to believe him.

On 15 August 1746, at Chelmsford, he was brought to the bar before Sir Michael Foster, Judge of the Assize. As a minor celebrity in the County of Essex, his trial attracted a great many people to the court, and it was reported that throughout the trial he behaved with great modesty and decency.

Confidently, Skinner pleaded not guilty to the indictment. Perhaps he was relying on people's memories being hazy after two years, in which case he was unaware of the affidavits that had been so fully recorded only three days after the shooting. Mr Page the victualler gave evidence of Skinner's impassioned threats to murder Brett. The prisoner's counsel asked if the deceased was not

(5)

the fame Day, her Mafter came home to his Houfe, ftanding on a Heath called the *Old Heath*, in the Parifh of St. *Giles*, in *Colchefter* ; it being reported to him that he had loft fome Goods, he flew in a Paffion, and faid, that he would have his Goods again, for he had ventured his Life for them once, and would venture his Life again for them, for that he would either Kill or be Killed; that he called for a Dram, which fhe gave him, and immediately thereupon he went out of the Houfe, mounted his Horfe, and rode off about half an Hour after Eight at Night : And that (as fhe believes) about three or four Hours afterwards, the faid Mr. *Skinner* called to this Examinant, and told her, fhe muft get up this Minute, which fhe did, and came to the Window, and defired him for Gods fake to tell her what was the Matter. He fpeaking in a Hurry, and feemingly confufed, faith, that he then made no Anfwer, but turned from the Houfe, and rid full Speed towards *Colchefter*, but for what fhe could not tell. Saith, that after fhe did come down fhe alighted a Candle, and renewed her Fire to fit by, expecting that he would come home again foon after: But faith, that her Mafter was not long gone from her the laft Time before the faid *Daniel Brett* came into the Room (where this Examinant was) all bloody. That

Deposition of witness against John Skinner. (The Life and Behaviour of John Skinner)

a smuggler, to which Page, who may have had his own reasons for a sudden loss of memory, replied cautiously, 'He may be a smuggler for ought I know'.

Mr Rallet the tailor stated that he had seen Skinner load a pistol and carbine at his house then leave in a great rage vowing speedy revenge against Brett. Several other witnesses were called, all of whom were able to prove premeditated malice against the deceased. One of the principal witnesses was reputed to have had a personal reason for wanting to see Skinner hang – the handsome smuggler had enticed his wife away. Skinner continued to use the lame story that he had acted in self-defence and called some character witnesses, who testified that they knew him as a quiet, peaceable man, but this was hardly proof of innocence. Some of them had only known him a short while, and were unable to speak of his behaviour in the past, so their evidence carried very little weight. The one witness notable by her absence was Miss Cooper. It was suggested that this was deliberate, as she would have been able to confirm that she had told Skinner that Brett had taken his goods, thus supplying the motive for murder, and she may have absented herself either from loyalty or at her master's instigation.

Inevitably the jury found Skinner guilty of the murder, and as it was the only capital conviction in court, he was at once brought to the bar to receive his sentence, which was death by hanging. The judge made a moving speech of which there is no detailed record, but he must have reproached Skinner not only with his guilt in the murder but also his life of dissolute conduct and crime. Skinner had probably never been spoken to like that before and seemed very shocked. The desperate nature of his situation now came to him with full force and he was observed to shed tears, whether of remorse or self-pity no one will ever know.

He was taken back to prison, and was from then on watched with very much greater care than before, for he was known to be a resourceful man with associates of bad character who might very well have arranged a daring escape. The strict watchfulness made him uneasy, and he raged at his keepers, as the contemporary writer of *The Life and Behaviour of John Skinner* recorded: 'You need not look so sharp after me, for I don't want to run away!' He continued to deny that he had had any premeditated malice against Brett, and appealed to everyone who had spoken to the stricken man asking if Brett had ever charged him with murder. It was true that Brett had never done so, but notwithstanding the sworn affidavit of Miss Cooper there were those who would testify that the reason Brett had made no such allegation was that he was scarcely able to speak, and when he did, it was only in broken words, which were hardly intelligible.

Some of Skinner's smuggler friends came to visit him in gaol, and he was in a good position to offer them valuable advice. According to *The Life and Behaviour of John Skinner* he told them 'never to trust their Servants with their Secrets, especially to keep them ignorant where their Goods were deposited; because, (said he) if you don't submit to their Humours, they'll not only inform against you, but rob you of whatever they can.' He added that the King lost more duties annually by lace-smugglers than all the smugglers in the kingdom beside, and he was sure that more French laces were annually worn in the three kingdoms than paid duty in ten years. The business of smuggling was also, he revealed, more than just a matter of goods. He said that since the French war, smugglers had also carried intelligence on events in the kingdom and what shipping was being fitted out, for which they were amply rewarded, and they always had free liberty to land in any port they wished.

Before the judges left Chelmsford the calendar was sent to the Sheriff, and he advised the keeper of the gaol that Skinner's execution was to be on 29 August. When Skinner was told of this he seemed much shaken, but remained hopeful of a reprieve. Friends prepared a petition and delivered it to the judges, and application was made to the King, but all to no avail.

Skinner now tried a new tactic. There was no more misplaced confidence, no more rage. He put on a melancholy face, took to praying long and intently, listened carefully to the priest sent to counsel him, and stated piously that he would much rather die than live. Often he would pretend to be ill, and sigh that he wished only for death, and for the happy day that would finally release him from his troubles. No one really believed either in his indisposition or the sudden change of heart. It was generally thought to be a pretence by which he hoped to obtain some special treatment from his gaoler which would facilitate his escape. He continued to be watched just as carefully as before.

Whatever one might say of Skinner, who was a scoundrel on many fronts, he was not as it turned out, lacking in physical courage, and he was not afraid to die. His real dread was of being hanged before a jeering crowd. He spent some of his last hours in writing, and this included a letter to a London friend, a copy of which was preserved. It was never intended to be published, and when it was made public after his death, certain names were omitted to protect the individuals named. It should not be surprising that in this letter – the text of which is given below in the original spelling – Skinner should reveal that his unhappy position was all the fault of other people.

My dear Friend

All that my Friends can do for me cannot save me; and I am greatly shock'd at my approaching Fate, because I no more expected to die for Daniel's Affair than you did. It's all the Doings of Tom P——, and that Rogue ——. I was bewitch'd to come home, for you know you always persuaded me to stay on t'other Side of the Water, or to keep in London. That Man who meddles with another's Wife is sooner or later brought to Destruction – You know what I mean; – that Jobb has brought all this Misery upon me. – What a terrible Shock it is for me to lay here in Irons, within a few Hours of Death, when you know how genteely I have liv'd in the World? Here's an end of all my Equipage and Grandeur, and poor Skinner is no more. To be exposed to a gazing Mob of Rabble, and unthinking silly people, has a greater Effect on me than Death, and I could wish to die in the Goal where I am. – I suppose Mr G—— and Tom W——s have heard of this, for I have read it in the Colchester and Ipswich News-Papers, and I know that Tom has them always sent over to him. – I don't expect any of my Acquaintance to come to see me, nor do I desire any, because my Time is so short; therefore God bless you and yours,

Your dying friend
J Skinner

Chelmsford Prison,
Aug. 21 1746

On the morning of the execution, the keeper of the prison went to advise Skinner that he must prepare himself for death, only to find that his charge had taken matters into his own hands. Blood was saturating Skinner's clothes, and pooling in the room, and the prisoner, while still alive, was weak and in great pain, though it was not immediately obvious what had caused his injury. A surgeon was sent for at once, and on searching the prisoner, it was found

THE
LIFE *and* BEHAVIOUR
O F
JOHN SKINNER,

Who was Executed *Auguſt* 29, 1746, at
CHELMSFORD in *ESSEX*
F O R   T H E
Murder of DANIEL BRETT,
(his late Servant) the 23d of *May*, 1744.

C O N T A I N I N G

I. A true Account of his Birth, Family, Education, and being put Apprentice to an eminent Oilman near St. Andrew's Church in Holborn.

II. His Marriage to a young Lady of good Family and Fortune in Eſſex, and ſetting up for himſelf without Aldgate; with the gay Manner in which he liv'd.

III. His cruel Uſage to his Wife, whoſe Company he deſerted for the Sake of Town Ladies, ſo that ſhe was obliged to go into the Pariſh Workhouſe.

IV. His becoming a Bankrupt, and retiring to Rumford, where he kept an Inn, and afterwards commenc'd Smuggler.

V. His ſhooting his Servant, for which he fled; his being apprehended; Commitment; Copies of the Affidavits made relating to the Murder; and his Trial at the Bar.

VI. His Deportment under Condemnation; a Letter to his Friend; and how he ſtabb'd himſelf the Morning of his Execution, to avoid a ſhameful Death.

VII. His Advice to all the Smugglers; his Behaviour and dying Words at the Place of Execution.

L O N D O N:

Printed for J. Thompſon, Publiſher, near the Seſſions-Houſe in the Old-Baily; and may be had at the Pamplet ſhops and of the News-ſellers. [Price Three-pence.]

Contemporary pamphlet on the life of John Skinner. (The Life and Behaviour of John Skinner) that Skinner had attempted to take his own life by stabbing himself. The knife he had used was so small, that having run it into his stomach with great force, it was wholly inside his body, handle and all. How he had obtained the knife was not known, perhaps it had been passed to him by a friend, for it seems unlikely that he had been permitted to have one in his cell.

Was the method of this botched attempt deliberate? In some ways, the location of the deep wound, and the slow agony experienced by Skinner in his last hours, mirrored the circumstances of Daniel Brett's unpleasant death. With great difficulty, the surgeon extracted the knife from Skinner's stomach and sewed up the wound. The prisoner, who was barely able to walk, was then led to church assisted by two of the keeper's men, where he heard prayers, and was then taken to the gallows. Skinner's worst fear, a large rabble of spectators assembled to see him die, was realised. He made no speech to them – even had he wanted to, he was in too much pain to speak. A short prayer was said, and Saucy Jack made his exit from the world.

The body of Colchester Jack – merchant, innkeeper, smuggler, murderer and ladies man – was loaded ignominiously onto a cart and taken to be buried in the village of his birth.

2

ONE NIGHT IN WALTHAMSTOW, 1751–2

In the eighteenth century a wealthy London businessman seeking a pleasant country retreat within easy commuting distance of his duties in the metropolis needed to look no further than Walthamstow. This largely rural community boasted many handsome manor houses in their own grounds, as well as humbler but still desirable residences with extensive gardens. A healthy place to live compared with the already polluted city, and situated close to the bucolic pleasures of Epping Forest, Walthamstow was also an excellent location to spend one's retirement. Joseph Jeffryes was a successful London butcher who had amassed a considerable fortune, possibly from cattle fattened on Walthamstow's ample pastures. Born in 1695, he had by 1729 acquired the tenancies of four properties and two parcels of land in Walthamstow, in the popular area of Wood Street, where his little enclave of houses later became known as Jeffries Square. Soon there were six houses in the square, five of them tenanted, the other occupied by Jeffryes, who also had the enjoyment of an orchard, and two acres of land. He owned in addition, the leasehold of a house in London, and an enviable assortment of household goods, not to mention valuable jewellery and a small fortune in cash. Early retirement beckoned, and the Jeffryes household moved to Walthamstow for good.

In the midst of plenty, Jeffryes had lacked one thing – an heir. He had adopted his brother's daughter Elizabeth when she was only five, and in 1746 drew up a will leaving her the bulk of his property. By 1751 she had grown into a bouncy miss of twenty-five, described by a contemporary observer as having 'a blooming Complexion, and a pretty good Shape, but a little inclined to Fat'. Elizabeth, not needing to soil her plump fingers with labour, was happy to enjoy the confidence and generosity of her uncle, and soon developed an unfortunate taste for strong drink, vulgar companions and pre-marital intimacy. Aware of his strict disapproval of this behaviour, she often persuaded neighbours to take him out for a walk, and ply him with liquor, so she could entertain her friends unhindered. Not that he was averse to the odd dram – his attendance at local hostelries was usually followed by the requirement for his general servant, John Swan, to bring him safely home. His favourite watering-hole was the Bald-faced Stag at Buckits Hill

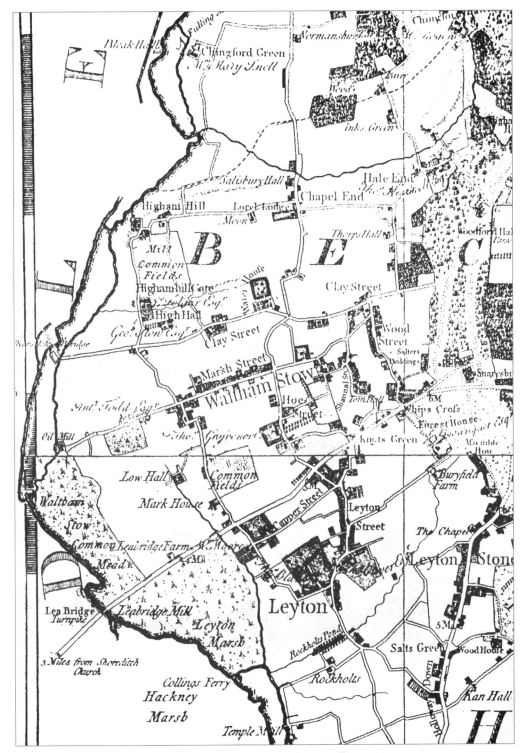

Walthamstow in 1777. (Author's Collection)

(now Buckhurst Hill) some 4 miles away. On one such visit, Jeffryes had fallen from his horse into a pond and Swan had rescued him.

Swan, a tall handsome fellow of twenty-seven, was the son of a Cambridgeshire brick maker, and a widower with a small daughter. Honest and trustworthy, he had been an exemplary servant to Jeffryes for three years. If he had faults it was a tendency to become aggressive when drunk, and a susceptibility which had made him Elizabeth's lover within a short time of their meeting. Jeffryes had noticed that the pair spent time together in the garden, though it is not certain if he was aware of how far matters had gone, and he had made his disapproval very clear. Virtue, for Elizabeth, was by then a distant memory. Some years previously there had been a disputed incident in a tavern with a young captain of the foot guard. The captain asserted that she was a bold miss who had enticed him there, and suspecting it was not safe to have connection with her, he had made his excuses and left. Elizabeth, finding she needed to explain her long absence from home, had accused him of rape. There was a confrontation before a magistrate, who, detecting that Jeffryes was mainly interested in extracting money from the captain for a promise not to prosecute, dismissed all three of them in disgust.

Elizabeth was naturally anxious to see off any possible rivals for her inheritance. Another niece had come to live with them, but Elizabeth had used her position of authority to ensure that the interloper was employed in menial duties, and she departed. In recent years however, a new danger threatened. Mr Jeffryes' deceased wife had been a widow, with a family by her previous marriage, and there was a grandson who was becoming a particular favourite. With Jeffryes still in good health and only in his fifty-sixth year, the money was far from being in the bank. The awkward situation limped along in an uncomfortable equilibrium. It only needed a catalyst, and this arrived in June 1751.

Jeffryes had been passing through Epping Forest with a cart when it became stuck in the road. As he struggled to free it, he was approached by a ragged and destitute man, called Thomas Mathews, who was on his way to London to look for work. Mathews had travelled, on foot, all the way from Hull. After helping to free the cart, Mathews explained that he was in some financial distress, and Jeffryes very kindly took him home and offered him a few days' work in return for his food and drink. When Mathews left Jeffryes' employ, nine days later, he was given 1s, but instead of leaving the neighbourhood, he found work with Mr Hughes, a farmer who lived in Wood Street. Mathews and Swan, who were perhaps not the most likely of friends, nevertheless continued to meet regularly to drink at Swan's expense.

On the 19 June Swan and Mathews joined Thomas Smith, a shoemaker, at the Green Man and Bell, Whitechapel, called for some bumbo, a kind of rum punch, and drank steadily from six in the evening till about ten, becoming sufficiently rowdy that the landlord, Mr Gall, came to see what was going on.

Suspicious of Mathews' ragged appearance, he was about to turn him out of the house, when Swan took off his coat, threw it aside, and said, 'Damn me, if you use my friend ill, I'll fight you!'. Swan's coat landed in the fire, and when Gall picked it out, he found it was heavy, felt in the pockets and discovered two pistols. Afraid that the men might be robbers, he at once called the Watch, and the two revellers found themselves locked up for the night. The next morning they were brought before the magistrate, Sir Samuel Gower, who committed them to the Bridewell in Clerkenwell, but advised Gall to send to Walthamstow to check Swan's story that he was in service with Mr Jeffryes. Gall went to Walthamstow himself, and saw Elizabeth, who hired a coach for the day and went to London. An accomplished liar with many years of practice, Elizabeth appeared before Gower and told him that the pistols belonged to a gentleman and she had sent Swan to town with them to get them cleaned. Swan and Mathews were duly discharged, and all three, together with Thomas Smith, brazenly went back to Mr Gall's and dined there. Mr Jeffryes was extremely displeased when he heard of the incident, and it took all Elizabeth's powers of persuasion to get him to allow her lover to come back. Mathews spent the next few days in nearby Epping, but by the end of June he was back in Walthamstow.

On Tuesday 2 July, the night of Joseph Jeffryes' death, the household consisted of Jeffryes, Elizabeth, Swan, the maidservant and a child, probably the cherished grandson. Many of the neighbours lived a matter of only a few yards away. There were, therefore, a substantial number of witnesses to the dramatic events. That evening there had been visitors to the house, and after they left, the doors and windows were fastened and the household retired to bed, everyone being in their rooms by midnight. The maid, Sarah Arnold, slept in the garret, but the other occupants were on the first floor, with Jeffryes and Elizabeth in adjacent rooms. At about quarter past two Mary Adams, who lived only twenty yards away, heard the sound of a pistol shot. She thought no more of the matter, but some three quarters of an hour later, there were screams of 'Fire! Thieves!', which roused her from her bed. Nearby, John and Elizabeth Diaper were also awoken by the screams, and jumping out of bed, opened the window to see the astonishing sight of Miss Jeffryes in her nightshift, halfway out of an upstairs window, screaming that there were rogues in the house. By the time the Diapers had thrown on some clothes and made their way downstairs, Elizabeth was in the courtyard, saying that she had jumped from the window, and injured her ankle. As the neighbours poured out of their houses she gasped that she had awoken from a dream to find her uncle murdered and had heard rogues running down the stairs saying they would set the house on fire.

Sarah Arnold, asleep in her garret, did not hear a shot but was awoken by the commotion. As she stared out of the window, astounded to see Elizabeth outdoors, barefoot, and in her nightshift, Swan came and told her he thought

Contemporary artist's impression of the murder of Joseph Jeffryes. (Authentick Memoirs of the Wicked Life and Transactions of Elizabeth Jeffryes, Spinster)

Jeffryes had been murdered. Sarah hurried to her master's bedroom. Jeffryes was not dead, but appallingly wounded. He lay in his bed, conscious, but unable to speak, blood congealing from gunshot wounds in his head, and a deep stab under one ear. A knife lay on the table beside him, although there did not seem to be any blood on it, and there were also the broken pieces of a gun that had exploded as it discharged. Sarah at once ran to get help.

Edward Buckle, awoken by the outcry, had been disinclined to stir from his bed until his wife told him Miss Jeffryes was running about in her nightshift, when he at once jumped up and hurried down to the courtyard to offer his assistance. Elizabeth begged him to attend to her uncle, and he went up to the bedroom. He found Jeffryes lying on his right side, and taking hold of the wounded man's left hand he spoke his name and asked if Jeffryes could signify that he understood. There was an answering squeeze of the hand. Richard Clark, hearing the outcry, ran into the courtyard, met Swan and asked what way the thieves had got in. Swan said he thought they had got in at the window and then out of the door, and Clark examined both door and window and looked all around the premises, both house and garden, but though there was dew on the grass, it seemed not to have been disturbed. Other witnesses observed that there was blood on the banisters of the staircase and on the stairs, as if someone had fled downstairs with bloody hands. Mrs Diaper came out and joined the crowd around Elizabeth, who begged her to help her uncle. After arranging for the maid to take the child to a neighbouring house, Mrs Diaper joined the group by the bedside. There was little that could be done for the stricken man. He was lifted up and supported with a bolster, and a doctor was sent for. Elizabeth had by now arrived in her uncle's room and knelt on the floor, imploring 'Dear Uncle if you can speak, speak to me!'. He was unable to do so, and squeezed her hand, but she gave way to such hysterical shrieks that she was sent downstairs again.

While Elizabeth was busy making a drama out of a crisis, Swan had gone to get help. Thomas Forbes, an apothecary of nearby Woodford, was called out of bed by Swan saying that a sad accident had befallen his master. Swan then hurried away to get a coach, saying he was going to London to find a surgeon. He stopped at a number of hostelries on the journey, for when the coach returned some hours later, Swan was lying in the bottom, drunk.

When Forbes cast his professional eye over Jeffryes' wounds he observed two given by a gun on the left side of his face and a stab wound near the ear. Probing the wounds he found the stab to be four inches deep. The wounds had been received some time before, as the blood was congealed, and all of them he regarded as potentially fatal.

James Thornton, a surgeon of Walthamstow, arrived soon after the alarm had been given, and stated that he thought the shooting had taken place an hour before. Interviewing Elizabeth, she said that she heard four fellows running down the stairs, cursing and swearing. One of them had said 'Damn it now we have done all the mischief we can, let us set the house on fire'. At this, she said she had jumped out of bed and given the alarm.

Some hours later, with her uncle still speechlessly holding onto life, Elizabeth, in a calmer mood, was able to say that certain goods had been stolen from the house, notably, a silver tankard, a silver cup and fifteen pewter plates. Bemoaning her uncle's fate, she asked Buckle if he would lay information so the villains could be caught. Buckle, already suspecting Thomas Mathews, said he would apprehend him if he found him, but this seemed to frighten Elizabeth who replied, 'Mr Buckle, don't meddle with him, for you'll bring me into trouble, and yourself too in so doing.'

Meanwhile, a great deal of evidence was accumulating to indicate that the murder had been an 'inside job'. Mr Hillier, a local farmer, had arrived at the house some hours after the murder, and joined the throng. He saw that a bar that had been used to secure the window had been removed and was standing by the door, also some of the lead from the window had been untwisted, but again, this had been done from the inside. 'From thence I apprehended that some of the family had done the murder,' he later said in court. Suspicion arose that the missing plate was not far away, possibly as close as the bottom of the garden pond. Hillier obtained some rakes, and organised a party of men to drag the pond. Soon afterwards, a dripping sack was hauled up containing pewter, brasses, a silver tankard and some spoons. Sarah Arnold also declared that the weapons used in the murder originated from within the house; in particular there had been a pair of pistols hanging up in the kitchen, one of which was missing. Further examination revealed that the wire which connected a bell in Jeffryes' room to the maid's room had been cut, revealing both premeditation and a knowledge of the household arrangements.

Jeffryes was never able to speak or indicate who had shot him. Asked to hold up his hand if he knew who had murdered him, he did not do so, although he was able to wipe his nose with a handkerchief. He lingered on until the evening and died at 8 p.m.

The big question was who had fired the fatal shot? The explosion of the murder weapon meant that whoever had fired the shot should have had a wounded hand. Neither Elizabeth nor Swan had any injury to their hands, and neither had a spot of blood on their persons. There was one suspect left – Thomas Mathews – and he had vanished.

Three days after Jeffryes' death, Elizabeth went to London to prove her uncle's will. Apart from £500 to his nephew Joseph (£1 in 1751 had the purchasing power of £108 today) and some trifling amounts to other relatives, the whole of his fortune came to Elizabeth. Her previous extravagances, tempered as they had been by the necessity of staying within the allowance granted by her uncle, were as nothing to the life she now began, but her freedom was short-lived, for suspicions were such that both she and Swan were soon taken to Chelmsford gaol. The keeper

Parish church, Walthamstow, 1783. Joseph Jeffryes was buried here. (Author's Collection)

having no authority to prevent them drinking or spending what they liked, he saw that Swan, whose board was paid for by Elizabeth, behaved himself well, while she drank excessively, played cards careless of how much she wagered, and cursed in a vindictive fashion against anyone to whom she had taken a dislike. Confident that she would eventually be free, she outfitted herself accordingly, with shoes at 25s a pair, and was having a new white calico dress made on which she spent £9. She had also bought a pretty white mare which she said she would ride out of Chelmsford when acquitted. The difficulty was that while there was ample evidence that the murder had not been carried out by intruders, there was no real evidence to show who the culprit was. It seemed that nothing could be resolved without Thomas Mathews.

In London, John Gall and Thomas Smith had not forgotten about Mathews, and on hearing that he was suspected of murder determined to watch out for him. Months passed, but on 9 November Smith spotted Mathews coming out of the offices of India House. Gall at once made enquiries, and found that Mathews had entered himself into the services of the East India Co., no doubt with the intention of going abroad. Learning where the wanted man was lodging, he at once arranged to have him arrested.

Mathews' first reaction was to deny that he was Thomas Mathews at all, and declare his name to be Smith, pleading utter ignorance of the murder of Mr Jeffryes. On being confronted with Mr Gall, he was obliged to confess to his real name, and this time stated that he knew who had committed the murder though he had had nothing to do with it himself. Brought before Sir Samuel Gower once more, he said that at the time of the murder he had been at sea, in the *Earnest Inquiry* and had been cast away on the Capes of Virginia. Asked about an injury to his hand he said it was a rope-burn. While Mathews languished in the Bridewell again, Gall made some enquiries and found that no such ship had been out in the last year. Dragged before Sir Samuel Gower, Mathews was obliged to admit that everything he had said before was a lie, and agreed to make a confession. The result was everything that Swan and Elizabeth had feared.

Mathews stated that about four days after he had started working for Mr Jeffryes, Elizabeth had asked him to go upstairs and clean some furniture, then quickly followed him up and as soon as they were alone, said 'What will you do if a person would give you a hundred pounds?'.

Somewhat taken aback, he responded that he was willing to earn such a sum if it was in an honest way, and Elizabeth told him to go and see Swan who would tell him what to do. Mathews went down to see Swan in the garden, and told him of the conversation with Elizabeth. Swan, smiling, drew him into an outhouse, and explained that if he, Mathews, knocked the old miser on the head, he would have £700. Elizabeth had joined them by now, and added that that she would not have a minute's sleep so long as her uncle was alive, since he had recently threatened to change his will.

About two days after Mathews had been discharged from Mr Hughes', Swan gave him half a guinea to buy some pistols. This was just too much temptation and Mathews spent the lot at the Green Man public house at Low Layton. He was headed for London when Swan overtook him. Annoyed at Mathews' failure to grasp the essence of what was required, he suggested they talk things over at the Green Man and Bell at Whitechapel, declaring in a fury that by God, if Mathews would not commit the murder then he would or somebody else must. Things were critical, since Elizabeth had told him she was pregnant, and if her uncle got to know of it she would be cut off from his estate and turned out of doors. (In the event it turned out that Elizabeth was not pregnant and this may very well have been a lie to firm Swan's resolve and hurry matters on.)

The two plotters had realised by now that they were not going to hold onto their man unless they came up with a constant supply of money, and so he was plied first with 1s and then half a crown. According to Mathews, (and this is the point in the story where Mathews' account and that of Swan and Elizabeth diverge) there was a meeting on the Monday before the murder, near the Buck in Walthamstow, and another at 2 p.m. the following day near the church, when Mathews was asked to come to the back door of Mr Jeffryes' house at 10 p.m. that night.

Mathews stated that he arrived as planned, and finding the door on the latch, entered, and hid behind a tub till eleven. Swan gave him some cold boiled beef to eat, then said that it was now time to knock the old man on the head. Having come this far, it seemed that Mathews now had an attack of conscience, and declared he could not find it in his heart to commit the crime. Elizabeth at once damned him for a villain, and Swan, who was holding two loaded pistols also damned him and said he had a great mind to blow his brains out. Instead, Swan produced a book and made Mathews swear that he would tell no one of what had passed. Swan and Elizabeth then both went up the stairs together. This was the point when any sensible man would have left immediately, but according to Mathews, he lingered downstairs, and about half an hour afterwards he heard a pistol go off. Only then did he hasten out of the back door.

No one seriously queried Mathews' account of the murder, which gave the authorities everything they needed to prosecute Elizabeth and Swan. On Wednesday 11 March 1752 the prisoners were brought before the Grand Jury at Chelmsford Assizes at 7 a.m. and both pleaded not guilty. The court was extremely crowded, and on the entry of the prisoners there was a great commotion, some spectators heaping reproach upon the accused, while others were moved to pity. Elizabeth, dressed in genteel mourning, showed very little emotion, possibly because she felt assured of an acquittal. 'One could read no malevolence in her countenance, nor indeed much sensibility,' wrote one onlooker, 'none of that which is inspired by dignity of thought, and conscious innocence, instead of which a kind of stupid inattentiveness sat on her features.' Due both to her sex and her station, she was permitted to sit.

The case for the prosecution was based on Thomas Mathews' confession, and there was ample support in the evidence of other witnesses. Sarah Arnold recalled seeing Swan cutting some lead bullets to fit the pistols, and the lead chippings were still lying on the kitchen floor after the shooting. She also confirmed Jeffryes' threat to cut Elizabeth out of his will for her loose behaviour.

William Gallant, a barber, testified that on the 25 June Elizabeth had asked him if he would take her uncle as far as Buckits Hill and keep him out till it was late, and make him pretty much in liquor, offering to pay him up to a crown (5s, the equivalent of £25 today) to do so. Gallant had declined this unusual request, claiming that he was busy. Elizabeth was not a woman to be denied. She caught him by the wrist and said, 'Dear Gallant, do it this week, if not this week, it must be done the next.' She then advised him that she would have money very shortly, and if he wanted any he could have 2 or 3 guineas.

One by one, the neighbours testified as to the events of the fatal night, and their suspicions that the murderer had been one of the household. The only emotion shown by Elizabeth was when Mrs Diaper fainted during her

Execute on Epping Forest, on Saturday ye 28 of March 1752. for being concernd with John Swan, in ye Murder of her Uncle, Mr. Jos.ͭ Jeffryes.

Elizabeth Jeffryes. (The Authentick Tryals of John Swan and Elizabeth Jeffryes)

testimony, upon which the accused took the opportunity of going into convulsions for fifteen minutes. The principal witness was Thomas Mathews, who while admitting that he had lied when first apprehended, stuck to his confession. The broken gun was a good point for the defence, although the counsel for the Crown expressed the opinion that due to its length it was possible for it to have been fired without causing injury. The judge summed up, and the jury withdrew, returning an hour later to find both the prisoners guilty.

The next day, while Swan declared to anyone who would hear him that Thomas Mathews had committed the murder, Elizabeth made a confession. She said she had been thinking of murdering her uncle for the last two years, but his threat to alter the will had finally determined her. Swan, as a loyal servant with no quarrel against his master, had been deeply shocked when she told him the plan, so she had added a lure. Although she had never intended to do more than live with Swan, preferring to be the mistress of herself and her fortune, she promised to marry him as soon as she had her uncle's property, ensuring financial security for his daughter. If Swan was still hesitating about killing an innocent man, she had another weapon in her armoury, accusations against her uncle of sexual abuse. Eventually, Swan agreed that Jeffryes should be murdered, and that a third party should be engaged to commit the crime. They felt sure that Mathews would be tempted because of his poverty, but he had done no more than drink their money and talk about it. Mathews, said Elizabeth, had told the truth about the plot, but he had not been in the house at the time of the murder – indeed she hadn't seen him for several days.

On the night of the murder, she and Swan had waited until her uncle and the maid were in their rooms, then she had helped Swan put the silver and pewter into a sack. They each fortified themselves with a dram of brandy then she retired to her room and waited for Swan to signal that the deed was done. She declared that she had fallen asleep, and knew nothing of the murder until Swan knocked on the door. After giving the alarm she had run downstairs and Swan had let her out into the courtyard.

When Swan discovered that Elizabeth had confessed, he was furious. When next permitted to speak to each other matters became somewhat heated and the keeper had to separate them.

On 14 March the prisoners were brought before the court and received their sentences – both were condemned to death, Elizabeth fainting away several times during the judge's speech. In the two weeks that remained to her, Elizabeth did everything in her power to excite compassion. She said that her uncle had debauched her when she was only fifteen, and that they had lived together in an incestuous relationship ever since. She had been pregnant on two occasions, the first ending in a miscarriage and the second when he

provided her with something to procure an abortion. Despite this, she later blamed the young captain as the man who had first ruined her. She then claimed that her uncle had recently transferred his affections to the maidservant and she had caught them in bed together. She had been impelled to kill her uncle because of his demands – he had insisted she go to bed with him on the very night of his death. Many people, she claimed, knew about her plans to kill her uncle because of the ill-usage she had suffered at his hands and also from Sarah Arnold, who had helped herself to her uncle's things, and was suspiciously well dressed on her pay of £5 per annum. It was a shocking tale of suffering and victimisation, the kind that people feel naturally inclined to believe, but somehow nobody quite bought it.

The next time Elizabeth and Swan met, Swan reproached her with being the cause of her uncle's death. He said she had promised to give his daughter £30 and asked if

John Swan in gaol. (The Authentick Tryals of John Swan and Elizabeth Jeffryes)

she would do so, but she confessed such a thing was not in her power. At this he became very distressed and said his daughter would be helpless and without support.

'You were as willing to do it as I!' she retorted.

'I would never have done it if it had not been for a reason you know,' he replied, referring to the supposed pregnancy. Again the keepers had to part them, and Elizabeth's two brothers took pity on Swan and promised him that they would give £30 to his daughter.

On Saturday 28 March the prisoners were prepared for their execution. At 5 a.m. Swan was put in a sledge, handcuffed and with irons on his legs and a halter around his shoulders. He was asked if Mathews had committed the murder but replied only that everyone would know the truth when he was dead. Elizabeth got as far as the handcuffs before she fainted again and four men were required to carry her to the cart that was to convey her. The procession set off. All the way, the roads were lined with people, and hedges and trees by the roadside were filled with spectators, as were the windows of nearby houses. After about a mile Elizabeth appeared to regain consciousness and asked for a religious book to read. One was borrowed for her, and she read as she sat. Some 8 miles from Chelmsford she put the book aside and fell into another fit, thrashing about in strong convulsions that lasted half an hour. Fortunately she was tied into the cart and there were people to hold her. Swan, though in a sledge was also able to read. At Brentwood they paused, and were given something to drink.

A curious misunderstanding seemed to have arisen concerning the location of the execution. The officials were in no doubt as to where it was to take place, the gibbet near the 6-mile stone in Epping Forest, just to the east of Woodford High Road. In Walthamstow, however, there was a strong conviction that the event was to take place opposite Mr Jeffryes' house in Wood Street, and with good reason, for a gallows had been built on the spot, though by whom, no one was able to determine.

Walthamstow seethed with excitement and expectation. People poured in to see the execution, on coaches, on horseback and on foot. A scaffold had been built around the gallows to give good views to those who were able to afford between 1s and 3s for a place. The fields all around were full of people, all of whom had paid something to the farmer for a place. Those with houses nearby that gave a prime viewpoint had let their windows, in one case for 5 guineas.

According to the official account of the case published by R. Walker, it had always been intended that the execution should take place in Epping Forest, and the population of Walthamstow had been deliberately misled by unscrupulous persons out to make a fast profit. The General Advertiser, however, based possibly on information given to their man on the spot, suggested that Walthamstow had been the original location, with Epping Forest only a secondary site for gibbeting Swan, and the location had been changed at the last minute when constables had been sent up ahead and on seeing the crowds had made a last minute change. Either way, the crowds were to be disappointed.

At 2 p.m. the little procession arrived at Epping Forest. The constables ringed the area, and the cart was drawn under the gibbet. While Swan was being removed from the sledge Elizabeth was asked if she truly repented. She said she did, though God alone only knew the ill-usage that had driven her to do what she did. Swan was brought up to the cart and shook hands with her before he got in. For half an hour prayers were said and both the condemned acknowledged the justice of their sentences. When Swan was asked if he had anything to add he began a tirade against Mathews who, he said, was a great villain, who had not only sworn what was false against him, but had also confessed to being involved in a notoriously brutal murder of two customs officers, Galley and Chater, for which a gang of smugglers had been hanged in 1749. Mathews had claimed to be the man who had slashed Galley's eyes out, though this was probably pure boastfulness, since it was Chater who had been blinded, and the identity of his attacker was known.

When the executioner put the hood on Elizabeth's head she swooned again. Swan was able to stand in the cart but she, being shorter, was placed on a chair. A prayer was said and the cart drew away. As the bodies swung, Swan's confession was read out. He had, he admitted, killed Mr Jeffryes alone by shooting him with a pistol loaded with pieces of bullets. Jeffryes, declared Swan, had never been stabbed – the numerous wounds came from the bullet pieces and the splinters of the bursting gun. Mathews had not been in the house for five days.

Meanwhile, back at Walthamstow, the crowd was getting restless. Those who had taken money for the prime seats were probably long-gone, and when the hearse that had been waiting ready to take the bodies drove away, it dawned upon people that they had been cheated. Confusion and disappointment gave way to anger, and the crowds in the fields demanded their money back, but the owners refused, saying they had been put to some expense themselves and their property damaged. This, commented the *General Advertiser*, 'occasioned a great disturbance and some mischief'.

Elizabeth's body was handed back to her relatives who arranged for her to be buried in Southwark. It was intended that Swan should be gibbeted where he hung, but as the place was in full view of some gentlemen's houses it was decided to take him to Buckits Hill and hang him near the Bald-faced Stag where he was so well known.

We may conclude that Thomas Mathews was not in this instance at least, a murderer – he simply strung the conspirators along with promises while they were willing to ply him with drink money. Once things heated up, he disappeared. Elizabeth and Swan had no reason to protect Mathews once he was arrested, and their confessions may be accepted. His story of being in the

AUTHENTICK

MEMOIRS

Of the Wicked Life and Transactions of

Elizabeth Jeffryes, Spinster.

Who was Executed on *Saturday*, *March* 28, 1752, on *Epping-Forest*, near *Walthamstow*.

For being concern'd in the MURDER of her late Uncle,

Mr. JOSEPH JEFFRYES:

WITH

The Particulars of her Behaviour, during the Time of her Confinement, before her Tryal; her Confession after her Conviction to the two Reverend Divines, Mr. *Tindall* and Mr. *Griffiths*; and of every Circumstance that Occured from the Time of her being acquainted that the Dead Warrant was come down, to the Time of her Execution.

ALSO

A Full Account of the *Life, Behavour*, and *Confession* of *John Swan*, who was Executed with her, for committing the said Murder.

LONDON, Printed and Sold by T. BAILEY in *Leadenhall-Street*, where Shopkeepers *Bills* are Printed at the *Letter* or *Rolling-Press* at Reasonable Rates.

1752

Contemporary pamphlet on the murder of Joseph Jeffryes. (Authentick Memoirs of the Wicked Life and Transactions of Elizabeth Jeffryes, Spinster)

house must have been a lie to strengthen the case against them, and divert suspicion from himself.

No one ever explained the long delay between the shots and giving the alarm – some three quarters of an hour – perhaps John Swan was waiting for Jeffryes to die, listening to his gasping breaths, unable to face what he had done.

And what of Elizabeth's claim that she did nothing but put some cups in a sack and was sound asleep when the crime was committed? Was it plausible that she had coolly fallen asleep while waiting for her uncle to be murdered in the adjacent room, and that she had not been awoken by a shot on the other side of a thin wall? And who made the blood smears on the banisters, which were supposed to suggest that intruders had been present? Perhaps her fine white hands were more involved than she would have us believe.

3

THE DAGENHAM
OUTRAGE, 1846–58

In the 1840s the rural village of Dagenham had a not undeserved reputation for lawlessness. While most of the population were agricultural labourers, growing wheat and potatoes, the location of the village, just 2 miles from the shores of the Thames estuary, encouraged a trend for supplementing meagre farm wages with smuggling. Between the village and the Thames was an area of desolate, windswept marshes, dotted with abandoned cottages, ideal for the concealment of contraband goods or as hiding places for some of the more desperate and brutal characters in the region.

There was no official Essex constabulary, and in 1840 it was decided to combat the problem by extending the Metropolitan Police to Dagenham. Men were drafted in to form a new force, which soon came into direct conflict with the criminal elements. The magistrates at the Ilford sessions were regularly required to hear charges of assault brought by the police against local criminals and sometimes, counter-charges made against the police. Such were the threats of revenge against local policemen that some of them had had to be removed from Dagenham to other districts and their places taken by newcomers. A typical confrontation occurred on 4 March 1846. PC Abia Butfoy was patrolling the road from Dagenham to the common when he encountered a man he knew to be of bad character, carrying a bag. Suspecting that the bag contained stolen property, he insisted on seeing its contents. The man refused and this resulted in a scuffle. Later the man showed him what was in the bag, but departed with a threat to get even. Butfoy continued on his beat without incident, but in mid-May it was felt that another man should take his place. That replacement was PC George Clark.

George Clark had been in the police force only six months, and in Dagenham just six weeks. He was twenty years old, robust and well able to take care of himself, and had already impressed his superiors with his conscientious attention to duty. He was a quiet, good humoured, religious lad, who sang hymns as he walked along and carried tracts in his pocket. He came from Battlesden, a village near Woburn, where his sweetheart, Miss Howe, resided. They had recently become engaged. Clark lodged at the police station, sharing a room with another young constable, James Stevens. Each night, the sergeant, William Parsons, marched his men out of the police station at about nine to do their night patrols. The station had only one horse and that was allotted to the sergeant who would patrol the area to ensure that his men were diligent in their duty.

The lone policeman walking country roads in the hopes of deterring a band of armed cut-throats was poorly equipped. He had a truncheon, and a cutlass and wore a thick greatcoat done up tightly at the neck with a stout leather stock to protect him against being strangled. If attacked, he could attempt to alert his colleagues with a wooden rattle. The rural police felt strongly that they should have been able to carry firearms, and the events of 29 June 1846 were to confirm many others in that belief.

That June had been one of the hottest and driest on record. Daytime temperatures had climbed to over 90°F, on Tuesday 29 June it had reached 78°, and the ground was baked hard. It must have been a relief to be on night duty. The nightly beat of the foot patrol from Dagenham police station started at a crossroads known as the Four Wantz, where the roads led to Ilford, Barking, Dagenham and Chigwell. There the men parted, each man setting off on his individual beat. They were due to meet up at set points and times during the night before returning to the station at 6 a.m. Clark was at his appointed place at 1 a.m., but two hours later, when expected to be between the Three Wantz (the meeting of roads leading to Dagenham, Barking and Ilford), and an area known as the Cottages, he was missing. When the men came off duty at six the following morning Clark was absent, and at this point there was very serious concern about his safety. Although his conduct had given every satisfaction, a letter was despatched to his mother to see if he had absconded to Battlesden to see his fiancée, but a reply came that he was not there. Over the next three days the search continued. The policemen paced out Clark's beat, and ponds in the vicinity were dragged for a corpse.

On the Friday night the police came to the cottage of Ralph Page, a local farmer, and asked his wife Elizabeth for permission to drag their pond. Mrs Page had not thus far seen fit to mention to anyone a curious incident that had taken place at 3 a.m. on 29 June. That night she had been awoken by the furious barking of her dogs, and had thought that she had heard a cry for help, but the barking was so loud she had not been able to make out

An 1840 cartoon showing contempt for the police. (Author's Collection)

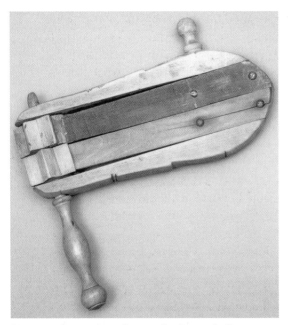

Nineteenth-century police rattle. (Essex Police Museum)

anything more distinctly. She had heard the following day about the missing policeman but failed to connect the two incidents. The pond having been dragged without result, Mrs Page told the policemen that there was another pond further on, and sent her two boys to show PCs Butfoy and Thomas Kimpton where it was. (Some writers have spelt this name 'Kempton' – here the spelling in the 1841 Dagenham census is used.) They were now some ¼ mile from the main road, and became aware of a strong smell. Looking around, Kimpton saw a policeman's staff, bloodstained, and very much cut about by some sharp instrument, and he immediately recognised it as the one carried by Clark. Going on a little further he found Clark's cutlass stuck in a hedge, and when it was withdrawn it was found to be covered in blood from the point to the hilt, with human hair sticking to it. Just half a dozen yards further on, was the body of George Clark, and even after the previous two discoveries he could not have been prepared for the ghastliness of the appearance of the corpse. 'Here he lies!' called Butfoy, while the children screamed so loudly their mother could hear them back at the farmhouse. Kimpton was too appalled to speak and Butfoy, who had a stronger stomach, added, 'you are a pretty cow-hearted sort of a policeman'. They at once called for Sergeant Parsons and James Stevens, who were in the adjoining field. Stevens took one look at the body and fell on his back in a dead faint.

George Clark was lying on his back in the wheat, one leg crossed over the other, one hand tightly grasping a handful of wheat in the last spasm of death. There had obviously been a fierce struggle, for the crops were trodden down to the extent of ten or twelve yards in every direction, almost as flat as if it had been rolled. The face and hands of the corpse were covered with blood and dirt. The wounds were appalling. There was a large opening in the back of the skull some six to eight inches in circumference. Part of the scalp was missing – it had been cut off, probably with the cutlass, and was lying beside the body.

The local surgeon, Mr Collins, was at once sent for to examine the body in place, then, about an hour after its discovery, it was decided to remove it to the ruins of a nearby cottage. The police borrowed a cart from Mrs Page, and she helped them put the body on it. It was clear that whatever the motive for the murder it could not have been robbery, for Clark's money and watch were found undisturbed in his pockets. His rattle was found still in his greatcoat pocket in such a position that he could not have got to it in time to give the alarm. Collins continued his examination, removing the leather stock which was completely saturated with blood, and found a deep wound to the throat, cutting through the windpipe and the root of the tongue almost through to the vertebrae. There was another wound under the right ear which went completely through the neck coming out on the other side, which must have been inflicted with a sharp, double-edged knife. Either of the neck wounds would have been instantly fatal. The face and chest were very bruised, but more detailed examination was not possible because of the advanced state of decomposition. There were other superficial wounds on the shoulder, and one finger had been cut off – probably a defence wound.

Late that night, Kimpton and two other policemen, one of whom was Stevens, brought the cart back to Mrs Page. They looked exhausted and she invited them in for some refreshment. Stevens was still feeling unwell and continually urged Kimpton to return to Dagenham. As they chatted, Kimpton mentioned that Sergeant Parsons had not been on duty on the night of Clark's murder. At about midnight, the Sergeant had said he was not feeling well and had asked Kimpton to take the horse and do his duty for him, which he did. This casual statement sowed the seeds of a major scandal which was to damage the reputation of the Metropolitan Police Force for several years.

With daylight, further searches were made at the scene of the crime, but there were no footprints to be seen, and though the wheat had been parted at the side of the field showing that people had passed that way, it could not be deduced from what direction they had come. At the murder site, broken pieces of Clark's skull were found so deeply embedded in the earth that they had to be dug out with a knife. The newspapers were to report that the body had been flung down with such force it had left an impression in the earth, but a more likely explanation was that Clark's corpse had been trampled into the ground by many feet.

On Saturday 4 July the inquest was opened, the jury meeting at a cottage not far from the Three Wantz. Although the time and place of the inquest had not been made public, such was the local interest that a large number of people had crowded there from the surrounding districts. The jury accompanied the coroner to the ruined cottage to view the remains, but the sight was so unpleasant that many could give the body no more than a cursory glance, and the smell made them feel nauseous and faint. Back at the temporary jury room the first person to be sworn in was Thomas Kimpton, who had marched out with Clark on the final beat. He had been due to meet up with Clark at the Four Wantz at 1 a.m., but Clark had not made an appearance. Abia Butfoy was sure he knew who should be suspected, and gave the court a name, but this was not made public.

MURDER OF A POLICEMAN.

DAGENHAM, SATURDAY EVENING, JULY 4.

A most atrocious murder was committed in the course of last week at Dagenham, in the county of Essex.

The following particulars, collected by the reporter on the spot where the murder took place, may be relied on as strictly accurate.

Since the extension of the metropolitan police to the rural districts of Essex, a very bad feeling has been shown towards them among the lower class of inhabitants of Dagenham, and a considerable portion of the time of the magistrates at the Ilford sessions has regularly been occupied in hearing charges of assault preferred by the police against persons residing in that locality, and counter-charges against the police themselves. This ill-feeling has arisen on account of the police by their vigilance having, on several occasions for some time past, succeeded in ridding this portion of the county of some very notorious characters. Some of the police, who had thus rendered themselves obnoxious, were, in consequence of various threats from time to time being held out to them, removed from Dagenham to distant stations, and their places supplied by others, among the latter being the deceased.

The unfortunate victim was a constable of the K division, named George Clarke. He was about 20 years of age, and had only been a short time in the force, and a few months stationed at Dagenham. His conduct had been most exemplary, and his steadiness appeared to give satisfaction not only to the police authorities but to the inhabitants of the village generally. On the 14th or 15th of May last Clarke was appointed to night duty on the beat where he met with his death, succeeding a constable named Batfoy, K 140, well known as being a vigilant officer. The beat commenced at a place called the Four Wants (cross-roads leading to Dagenham, Ilford, Hornchurch, and Chigwell), and extended a considerable distance along unfrequented roads, having deep ditches on either side, covered with duckweed, some parts of the beat being extremely lonely.

On Monday night last, at 9 o'clock, the deceased and three other men were marched from the Dagenham station to go on duty, the deceased being left as usual by his sergeant at the Four Wants. The following morning, at 1 o'clock, he was met by Sergeant Parsons, between the Three Wants (roads to Barking, Dagenham, and Ilford), and "the Cottages," that being the proper time for the deceased in accordance with his duty to be there. It was also his duty to have been at this spot at 3 o'clock the same morning, but on the sergeant's arrival there he was missed. After waiting some considerable time Sergeant Parsons returned to the station, and reported Clarke absent. At 6 o'clock on Tuesday morning, when the other men came off duty, the poor fellow was not among them, and then some

Extract from The Times *describing the murder of PC Clark. (The Times)*

William Parsons, the Dagenham station sergeant, now stepped up to give his evidence. Mrs Page was present to hear his testimony, though she was not questioned herself, and what he said must have left her feeling shocked and confused. Parsons said that after marching the men out he had left Clark at the Four Wantz at 9.20 p.m., but that he had later seen him at about 1 a.m. between the Wantz and the Cottages. Parsons said he had continued on duty until 3 a.m. when he should have seen Clark at the same spot, and on not seeing him, went around Clark's beat in search of him but did not find him.

The inquest was adjourned for a fortnight, and Clark's mother, who had travelled up from Battlesden, appealed to the court to be allowed to see the body. She had already asked the police, but in view of the nature of the wounds and the decomposition they had refused. The coroner observed that he did not have the power to prevent her but begged her not to do so. She entreated him again, as the deceased was her only son, and her request was finally granted. As anticipated, she was taken away from the sight in a state of insensibly.

As soon as the hearing was concluded, the police searched the murder scene again to look for the victim's hat which had not been found. It was finally discovered in the wheat some 12 to 14yd distant, where the crop was untrampled, suggesting that either it had been thrown there or had been knocked off his head by a blow.

Two detective officers from Scotland Yard arrived to conduct the investigation and they set about questioning all the inhabitants of the locality, making visits to the public houses and beer shops, while any notorious bad characters were placed under surveillance. The general opinion of those living locally was that Clark had been murdered in an act of revenge having been mistaken for Abia Butfoy. The body had been found at a point in the field where it was furthest from the three farms in the vicinity, and it was so far from his normal beat that he must have been deliberately lured there.

At the adjourned inquest Mrs Page now gave her evidence including the comments made by Kimpton about Parsons' absence from duty. However, when Stevens gave his testimony he stated that he had seen Parsons on duty at 12.45 a.m. at Broad Street 1 mile from the Four Wantz. He agreed that he had helped take the cart back to Mrs Page, but denied that anything had been said about Parsons not doing his duty on the night of the murder. Kimpton was questioned and denied having made the statement about Parsons. The coroner pointed out that Mrs Page had stated he had said so, but he continued to deny it. Mrs Page now confronted him, and declared that what she had said on her oath was true. Kimpton responded by swearing that he had himself seen Parsons on horseback doing his duty on the night in question. Another constable, Isaac Hickton, now took the stand and testified that he had also seen Parsons on duty. When Sergeant Parsons was called, he again said that he had last seen Clark at 1 a.m.

Mrs Page was adamant that she had been telling the truth, and was not prepared to let the matter rest. At the next hearing, her daughter Priscilla gave evidence. She had been present at the disputed conversation and testified that not only had Kimpton said that he had done Parsons' duty that night, but it had not been the first time he had done so. Mrs Page and Kimpton were then brought in to the court, and there was a testy confrontation, each sticking to their testimony.

A neighbour called Mr Kettle had also helped the police with the cart and had been present in the kitchen at the time of the conversation. Asked to testify as to whether the disputed statement had been made, he declared himself unable to remember. Mrs Page was heard to observe dryly that he had remembered it well enough last Saturday, and the jury expressed their strong opinion that the witness knew a great deal more than he was saying. James March, a labourer, was another who had assisted with transport of the body, and he testified that he had never heard Kimpton say he had done Parsons' duty. Unfortunately for March his employer was a member of the jury and he immediately pointed out that he had heard March saying he had heard this statement not once but several times.

Things were now looking so awkward that Parsons spoke up and said that it seemed they were trying to prove him the murderer, but claimed he could produce three or four witnesses who could contradict the statements that had been made. The coroner clearly didn't like his tone, and told him bluntly that he should be grateful to them for sifting the matter as it was due to his character that they should do so. By now it was painfully apparent that several people in court had lied, the only problem being determining exactly which ones.

A Dagenham grocer, Thomas Smith, supported Mrs Page by saying that when he had seen Kimpton at the Four Wantz with Clark's body, Kimpton had told him that he had done duty for Parsons on the horse.

Julia Parsons, the sergeant's sister, lived at Mile End but had been staying with her brother at the time of the murder, and it was hoped that her evidence would clarify matters. She said she had met up with Clark and Parsons at about 9 p.m. on the night of the murder, when she had been accompanied by Parsons' wife. Clark had been in a jocular mood, for when Mrs Parsons complained of feeling tired he had jokingly suggested he lift her onto the policeman's horse. They had returned home, and Clark and Parsons went on. She said her brother had returned to the station at midnight, had made out a report then gone out again. She had then gone to bed and did not see her brother till 9 a.m. the next morning, and was unable to say whether he had been home.

There were some further witnesses, but although it was not in dispute that Parsons was on duty up to midnight, the period after this remained in question. A witness named John Dale now testified that he had seen Parsons on duty on horseback between 3 a.m. and 4 a.m. The coroner remarked approvingly that this accorded with Kimpton's statement. In his opinion there was no doubt that Parsons had, as he and all the police had said, been on duty the whole night, and the only question was whether or not Kimpton had made the statement to Mrs Page. He believed that the evidence went to show that Kimpton had made it and why he had done so God only knew. In vain did Kimpton protest that he had not done so, for the jury said that they were satisfied that he did. The inquest was adjourned for a month.

It was clear that despite every effort of the police, there was no real evidence as to who had committed the murder, although it was felt that the culprits were local and the motive revenge. In August, out of a kind of desperation, a hearing was held concerning the potential involvement of three Irish itinerant agricultural labourers who had been taken into custody in Woolwich after a drunken altercation in which words had been bandied about concerning the murder of Clark. Nothing more was heard about this, but the hearing was to have remarkable consequences.

Abia Butfoy, having given evidence to the magistrates at Ilford concerning the labourers, had then returned to Dagenham, but on being required to go on duty, he was suddenly nowhere to be found. Perhaps as a result of having to air the whole story again, Butfoy had suffered a crisis of conscience. He had gone to Scotland Yard and there made a statement admitting that all the police had lied at the inquest and that Kimpton had indeed done Parsons' duty for him. As a result, officers were at once despatched to Dagenham and Sergeant Parsons and his constables were all taken into custody. All the police, Parsons and the five constables who had been on duty that night,

£100 Reward

WHEREAS on the Night of the 29th JUNE, or the Morning o' the 30th,

GEORGE CLARK,

Police Constable of the K Division of Metropolitan Police, was brutally Murdered, when on Duty, by some Person or Persons unknown, in a Field in the Parish of Dagenham, in the County of Essex,

A REWARD

Wanted poster for murderer of PC Clark. (London Borough of Barking and Dag

Old Dagenham. (Author's Collection)

Hickton, Kimpton, Stevens, Butfoy and Farns, were relieved of their duties and placed under surveillance.

The news caused considerable excitement not only in Dagenham and its nearby villages but caused ripples of astonishment all the way to London, concerning as it did the Metropolitan Police. It was widely rumoured that the men had been arrested for being connected with the murder. Since the young constable had been efficient, religious and popular, motives were hard to come by. Perhaps, it was hinted, his colleagues were jealous because he was just too efficient, religious and popular – perhaps he had discovered that they had been involved in smuggling or lectured them about their drinking habits, or maybe the incident with Mrs Parsons and the horse had aroused the Sergeant to a frenzy of jealousy. The suggestion that Clark might have been killed for the key to his box which contained some money foundered when it was discovered that the box was open. Ultimately, no evidence was ever produced that the police were involved in the murder of Clark, although many people believe it to this day.

At the resumed inquest excitement was at a pitch never before experienced, the court being crowded to suffocation with interested parties who stared at the two Scotland Yard superintendents who were present to watch the proceedings.

The constables, now in plain clothes, gave evidence, and admitted that they had lied when saying that they had seen Parsons on duty after midnight. They had lied because after the body was found, Parsons asked them all to say he had been on duty. They were, he told them, in a mess and needed to stick to the same story. In case they forgot what to say, Parsons had assisted them by calling them into a room and showing them a paper on which he had written the times when they were to say they had seen him on duty. Once the constables had told their story Parsons was called to give evidence and was adamant that his original story was correct and that all his men were lying.

A few days later on the night of 27 August the constables on duty at the Dagenham police station overheard a furious argument going on upstairs between William Parsons and his sister. Although the door was closed they heard Parsons threaten to throw her down the stairs if she did not hold her tongue. They clustered together at the bottom of the stairs to listen.

'You know you are guilty of it!' Julia was heard to say.

'In this affair?' replied Parsons.

'Yes and many more!'

Parsons then called her a name, which none of the constables wished to repeat, and burst out crying.

In September, while the weather continued warm, the attitude of the courts towards the police had turned distinctly icy. The inquest had to be adjourned due to the illness of one of the jurors and Mr Rawlings, Parsons' solicitor, complained about the hardship being experienced by his client. The coroner was curt. He said that Parsons had brought it upon himself by his own conduct and had no right to complain. The next time the court met, Julia Parsons was questioned about the quarrel, but denied it was anything to do with Clark's murder. After a lengthy summing up the inquest jury returned a verdict of 'wilful murder against some person or persons unknown'.

It was November before it was decided that since Butfoy, Farns and Stevens had not been under oath when first examined before the coroner the charge of perjury against them could not be sustained, and they were simply dismissed from the force. The others were suspended without pay while waiting to see if they would stand trial, and times were hard for them, especially Kimpton who was married with six children to support, and was obliged to apply for poor relief.

It was not until the following March that it was decided to proceed against Kimpton, Hickton and Parsons on charges of wilful and corrupt perjury, but when the three men were called before a jury to apply for bail, only one of them, Kimpton, appeared, Parsons and Hickton having made their own arrangements by absconding. In London and Essex there was the unusual sight of placards being posted offering a reward of £50 for the apprehension of the two former policemen. Kimpton required £400 in bail, which was not forthcoming, so he was taken to Ilford gaol.

£50 Reward.

WHEREAS

William Parsons,
a Police Serjeant, and

Isaac Hickton,
a Police Constable,

lately in the *K Division* of the Metropolitan Police, stand charged with Conspiracy and Perjury at the Inquest held at Dagenham, in the County of Essex, upon the body of GEORGE CLARK, a Police Constable, who was Murdered on the 29th June, 1846.

Her Majesty's Government

will give the above REWARD, to any Person who shall give such Information as will lead to the Apprehension of these Men, or a proportion of it for the Apprehension of either of them.

Description of Parsons,

Aged 30 Years, Height 5 feet 7½ inches, Fresh Complexion, small Grey Eyes, Sandy Hair and Whiskers, much freckled, walks upright, and is well proportioned, by Trade a Miller, Born in Saint Peter's, Norwich.

Description of Hickton,

Aged 33 Years, Height 5 feet 9¼ inches, Fair Complexion, Grey Eyes, light Brown Hair, small Sandy Whiskers, round Shouldered, draws his Mouth on one side when talking, especially when excited, by Trade a Currier, and was employed at a Tanner's at Hales Owen, near Birmingham, about 3 Months since, Born in Saint Warbus, Derby.

Information to be given at the Police Office, Great Scotland Yard, to the Police Station, K Division, Arbour-square, Stepney, or any of the Police Stations.

Metropolitan Police Office,
 4, Whitehall Place.

Wanted notice for the two absconding policemen. (Essex Police Museum)

Hickton, it was later found, had gone to Liverpool, but having seen bills issued for his and Parsons' apprehension his nerve failed him. As if he was not in enough trouble already, he decided in early July to write to his father asking to send Sergeant Hardy of the Derbyshire police force to arrest him. Hardy was an old school friend and Hickton wanted him to get the reward.

The charge of perjury was heard in July. Hickton felt very strongly about his situation. 'My lord,' he said, 'we screened the Sergeant in his neglect of duty and told a falsehood not knowing the consequences. The sergeants make a report and have us turned out of our situations if we do not say what they please to order.' He and Kimpton were found guilty and the judge, Mr Baron Parke, passed the maximum punishment for the offence, 'for if we cannot have truth from police officers what guarantee have we for the security of either our persons or property?' They were sentenced to a fine of 1s, prison for a week and then transportation for seven years. Hickton was sent to serve his sentence in Portsmouth dockyard and Kimpton on board a convict ship at Woolwich. Both men were pardoned in 1849.

In August 1847 a memorial was placed on the grave of George Clark, the inscription reflecting the feelings of the community. 'His uniform good conduct gained him the respect of all who knew him, and his melancholy end was universally deplored'.

Parsons, who was apprehended in Lincolnshire, stood trial in March 1848 for conspiracy to impede the course of justice. The judge commented on the generally excellent behaviour of the Essex police, and pointed out that since the perjury was clearly to avoid charges of neglect of duty and had nothing to do with hindering the investigation into Clark's death, he had not technically been indicted on the correct charge. Parsons was duly acquitted and walked from the court a free man.

Although local people had their private suspicions, no proof could be brought against any individuals, and there the matter rested until June 1858. Mrs Mary Ann Smith, who at the time of the murder had been Mrs Page (she was not related to the Page family near whose farm the body was found), now revealed that the murderous gang had consisted of her then husband William, and four other locals, Ned Wood (or in some accounts Wilcox), George Chalk, George Blewitt and a small farmer called Page who had carried out the murder after being surprised by Clark while stealing corn from a barn. She herself had been standing lookout and had given the alarm when she saw Clark approach. She had witnessed the start of the attack but had run home. William Page was killed in an accident about a year later, Wood was said to have hanged himself, Page had poisoned himself six years ago, and Chalk was in Australia. That left 32-year-old hay carter George Blewitt, who was at once arrested. Blewitt, clad in a long faded blue smock-frock appeared at the Ilford petty sessions in July, when it became apparent that there was a problem with Mrs Smith's story, and indeed, a problem with Mrs Smith. She had claimed that the murder had taken place near the barn which was being robbed and the body then carried to the spot where it was found. Questioning the witnesses to the discovery of the body confirmed that the area around it had been trampled from a violent fight, blood had pooled underneath where the body was located and there was no trail of blood nearby. There could be no doubt that the murder had taken place nowhere else but where the body lay. Mrs Smith was cross-examined and it seemed that she had got it into her head that Blewitt or some member of his family had stolen money from her. She also revealed that she was prone to having supernatural visitations and dreams, having several times seen her dead husband, and had also heard the devil tapping under her chair. Her neighbours, she said, whispered between themselves that she was 'not quite right', and by the end of her testimony, the court had come to much the same conclusion. 'The magistrates,' said Mr Atkinson for the defence, 'would not pull a feather out of a sparrow's wing upon such evidence as this.' It is unsurprising that later that month at the summer assizes the jury found 'no bill' against Blewitt who was at once freed.

Hope faded and memory faded. No one was ever convicted of the murder of PC George Clark, though the vicious characters who stabbed and trampled the young man, and cut the scalp from his head may well have paid the price for other crimes. The secret of who murdered Clark must lie not so much in the act of murder as the dreadful mutilations of his corpse, which can only have been carried out by those with a deep hatred either of the young man or what he stood for.

But PC George Clark was not entirely forgotten. On Sunday 30 June 1996 the 150th anniversary of his death was commemorated in Dagenham by a service held at the Church of St Peter and St Paul and a tree-planting at Eastbrook End Country Park. Policemen visited local schools to talk about policing in Victorian times, restoration work was carried out on the monument, and a letter from Police Commissioner Sir Paul Condon was presented to Clark's great-great-niece. Clark alone of all the men that night had done his duty to the end.

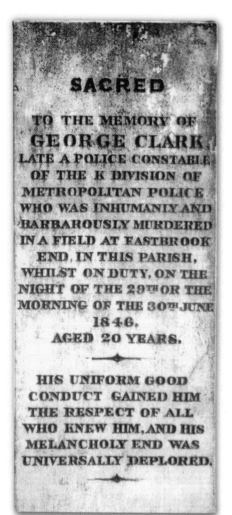

The monument to Clark. (London Borough of Barking and Dagenham)

4

THE CLAVERING POISONER, 1845–51

In August 1846 an unremarkable court case was to spark off a chain of events that resulted in the tiny rural village of Clavering becoming the centre of a national scandal. There would be four suspicious deaths, several trials, an execution and ultimately a change in the law governing the sale of arsenic.

In the 1840s Clavering was a village of approximately 1,000 people. The main wage-earning occupation was that of agricultural labourer, the principal crop being barley. The poorest families lived in small cottages with clay walls and thatched roofs, their ability to ward off starvation depending on the number of their children and the state of the harvest. Many were obliged to rely on poor relief. What passed for gentry in the area were the farmers who employed them. At Curles Farm, the Newports employed about fifteen men and boys, and theirs was one of the few houses in the area with servants. In the autumn of 1844 the Newport family (who were from Suffolk and unconnected with the Essex village of that name) consisted of John, fifty-two, his wife Susan, daughters Fanny and Mary Ann and their son, 26-year-old Thomas. That autumn they engaged a new maidservant, seventeen-year-old Lydia Taylor from the nearby village of Manuden. Both her wages and her absence must have been something of a blessing. Her father was a labourer and he, his wife and seven children occupied a small but cleanly kept hovel.

By the following spring Lydia was exhibiting the unmistakable symptoms of early pregnancy. Mrs Newport, in giving the girl her notice, asked who the prospective father was, and learned to her dismay that it was none other than her own son. Confronted with this, Thomas did not deny responsibility, but had an easy solution. He told Lydia he would get some medicine for her which would take everything away in a few days, adding that it would be better both for her and for him if she agreed. Angrily, Lydia said she would do no such thing. Thomas was not a man to take no for an answer, and the next day he came to her and asked again if she would take something. This time he had it in his pocket, and went to take it out, but before he could do so Lydia pushed him away. He walked off and she never spoke to him again.

In December 1845 Lydia, who had returned to live with her mother, gave birth to a healthy baby boy who was christened Solomon. Mrs Taylor went to see Thomas and asked him for money to support the child, which he grudgingly provided.

Old cottages, Clavering. (Author's Collection)

Early in 1846, Lydia was feeling unwell when she received an unexpected visitor. Sarah Chesham was the wife of Richard Chesham, a labourer of Clavering. Lydia barely knew her to speak to, yet suddenly the woman arrived at her house bringing a rice pudding, apple turnover, butter, tea and sugar. Lydia did not know it, but 36-year-old Sarah, a strong handsome woman and mother of six, had reputedly been having an affair with Thomas Newport. Sarah made a great fuss of the baby, and declared that Mr Newport was a good-for-nothing fellow. As she held the child in her arms she suddenly exclaimed, 'Lord, Lydia, it has turned as callow as a rat!' Lydia took the baby which looked very ill and saw that there was something white and slimy on its lips. She demanded to know what Sarah had given it, but Sarah said it was nothing but sugar. She left soon afterwards, and the child gradually recovered, but the family were afraid to eat any of the things she had brought and threw them away.

Sarah now bombarded the Taylors with requests for Lydia to come and see her and bring the baby. No doubt thinking that all would be well as long as she held the child in her arms, Lydia eventually gave in and paid Sarah a visit. As they were in one of the upper rooms of the cottage, Sarah looked out of the window, exclaimed that she saw Thomas Newport walking across the field, and said she wanted to take the child to see its father. Lydia refused, but to her horror Sarah snatched the child from her arms and ran down the stairs and out of the house. Lydia gave chase, losing sight of her quarry at first then finally catching up with her. Sarah was still holding the child but was wiping her fingers on her gown. The baby had been sick and there was something on its mouth resembling a pink ointment. Lydia snatched her child back and went home. Later it went into convulsions and was very ill for three weeks.

A few weeks later, Lydia weaned the child so she could leave it with her mother while she went into service with a Dr Welch at Stansted. The very next day Sarah Chesham was back at Manuden. Mrs Taylor, possibly hoping to escape Sarah's attentions, said she was going out, but Sarah accompanied her, took the baby and quickly ran around the corner. Mrs Taylor ran after her and turning the corner saw Sarah with one foot on the bank, the child on her arm and knee, putting something in its mouth. Mrs Taylor accused her of poisoning the child and snatched it back, taking it home. Once again the child was very ill and from that time onwards its health declined steadily.

By August, the once thriving Solomon was a very sick little boy, and Thomas was failing in his promise to provide support for his son. This gave the Taylor family the opportunity to air their grievances on a wider and more public stage. Thomas Newport was summoned to a hearing of the Saffron Walden petty sessions, where the magistrates made an order for him to contribute 2s 6d per week (equivalent to about £7 today) towards the support of his child. At the same time, Lydia's mother produced a letter from Mr Bowker, a Bishop's Stortford solicitor, the effects of which were to prove explosive.

Old Cottages, Manuden. (Author's Collection)

The letter was never published but the effect of it was to accuse Sarah Chesham of being the agent of another person in an attempt to murder the child. The magistrates were told that Solomon had been healthy when born, but they could easily see that the child lying in its grandmother's arms was thin and sickly. They at once made an order for Superintendent Clarke of the Newport division to make enquiries. Sarah was taken to Newport police station where a lengthy investigation was made behind closed doors, after which she was placed in Springfield Gaol. A search was made of her house and numerous items were removed.

The condition of little Solomon was not the only matter engaging people's attention. It was recalled that in January 1845 two of Sarah Chesham's own children had died under alarming circumstances. Joseph, born in 1834, and James, born in 1836, had both been taken very ill with symptoms of stomach pains and vomiting which the local doctor had attributed to cholera. If, as it now seemed, Solomon had been poisoned, could it be that Sarah had murdered her own children as well?

Soon the news spread that the bodies of Joseph and James Chesham were to be exhumed. The vicar of Newport saw the bodies, and although they had turned black, the features were sufficiently preserved that he could recognise them, and was able to point out which one was Joseph. The stomachs were taken to London for analysis where they and the medicines found in the Chesham house were examined at Guy's Hospital by Professor Alfred Swaine Taylor, the original editor of the standard textbook *Principles and Practice of Medical Jurisprudence*.

On 4 September a large but quiet and orderly crowd gathered around the Fox and Hounds Inn where the inquest was to be held, and inside the proceedings were watched by such respectable persons as the vicar of Clavering and several magistrates of the county and resident gentry.

Professor Taylor stated that the boys' stomachs contained an amount of arsenic that would have been fatal to an adult and in both cases it had clearly been introduced during life. He had no doubt that the cause of death was arsenical poisoning.

A vital witness was Thomas Deards, a painter, who that January had lived next door to the Cheshams. The families were separated only by a thin wall, and the upper room in which the boys slept projected for 3 or 4ft over the lower room of Deards' house. He had seen Joseph on Friday 17 January and the boy appeared to be perfectly well, but early the next day Deards was told by Sarah Chesham that Joseph had been taken very ill. She said that as Joseph was on his way home the previous night he had been met by Thomas Newport who had struck him with a stick, and she was afraid that he had hurt his insides. Deards sensibly told her to call in the local doctor, and she said she would, but when he came home that evening, no doctor had been sent for, and James, who no one ever suggested had been hit by anyone, was also ill.

Richard Chesham had been out since early on Saturday. Returning late, and finding two of his sons in bed and vomiting, he went at once to see Mr Hawkes, the local surgeon, and told him the children were very ill. Hawkes later claimed that he had offered to come and see the boys but that Chesham had said it was not necessary, a comment which Chesham was later to deny. A bottle of medicine was sent, the main ingredient of which was calomel, a laxative. It is not known if the boys were ever given this medicine or if they did whether they were able to keep it down.

That night Deards heard groaning noises coming from the Chesham house, and in the morning he heard both of the boys vomiting. He was at breakfast when vomit poured between the cracks of the boards above, and onto his table and the floor. He went to chapel and when he came home at 12.15 p.m. he could still hear the boys vomiting. He tried the Cheshams' door but was unable to open it. Going out, he was astonished to meet Sarah in the street. 'Mrs Chesham, are you aware how bad your children are?' he exclaimed. Referring to the vomiting he added, 'We can scarcely live in the house!' Her reply was, 'I will go home and alter it.'

Deards again went to chapel but when he came home at 4 p.m. found the vomit coming through the floorboards just as bad as before. He could hear the children vomiting, Joseph on one side of the bed, James on the other. He remained only a short time, and going into the village, again saw Sarah Chesham in the street. He marched up to her. 'Mrs Chesham, your children are very bad and there is no-one at home to attend to them,' he said. 'Had you not better let Mr Hawkes see them?' She promised she would.

Deards heard nothing more from the children, and went to bed at 9 p.m., but soon afterwards Sarah Chesham knocked on his door calling 'Master Deards, get up for God's sake, for my child's dying!' Deards got out of bed and went next door. Sarah Chesham's sudden attack of concern for her children had come a little late. Joseph lay on the bed, having just expired, with James, very ill, beside him. Deards assisted with the laying out, and saw that Mrs Chesham appeared distressed, as she held a handkerchief over her face. The following morning Richard Chesham again went to see Hawkes and told him that one of his sons was dead. Hawkes, now realising that the matter was serious, went to the Cheshams' house, and found James weak and in great pain. He again prescribed a laxative. Although he had not examined Joseph while alive he took the view that the death was due to cholera, even though it was an unusual season of the year for this to be the case. Later in the day James grew weaker and was prescribed opium and calomel. Hawkes' last visit was at 7 p.m. when the patient had declined further. The following day, Tuesday 22 January, he was told that James had died.

Hawkes had suggested a post mortem examination, but Sarah was reluctant to give permission, so nothing more was said about it. He certified both the deaths as due to cholera. On Saturday 25 January 1845 the two children were

The Fox and Hounds, Clavering. (Author's Collection, by kind permission of the landlord)

buried at Clavering churchyard. At the request of their mother they were placed in the same coffin.

Two villagers who had arsenic for the purposes of pest control testified at the inquest that Sarah Chesham had asked them to let her have some. Both denied that they had supplied her with arsenic.

There was another person with ready access to arsenic and that was Thomas Newport. He testified that he had bought some three years ago, but Sarah Chesham had never asked him for some and he had never given her any. He admitted striking Joseph, but in December 1844. Joseph had worked for him two years and he had discharged him after finding two stolen eggs in the boy's pocket.

Thirteen-year-old John Chesham, the dead boys' brother, gave evidence, but it was felt by the court that he had been tutored by someone to know as little about the matter as possible. He denied ever being given food by his mother that he could not eat, yet his employer stated that when Joseph and James had been ill, John had shown the same symptoms. He had given him gin to drink and sent him home.

The inquest was adjourned for a fortnight, and reconvened on 18 September at the Fox and Hounds when fifteen-year-old Phillip Chesham, Sarah's oldest son, gave evidence that there was no arsenic in the house. Like John, he denied being ill at the same time as his brothers, apart from having a headache. It had been rumoured that his mother had given him food which he had fed to his dog, which afterwards died, but he said he had never given the dog his food.

The question then arose of whether John Chesham had been told what to say at the previous hearing. A Mrs Green stated that she had heard John Chesham say that his master had told him what to say at the inquest. A local man, Charles Cole, who worked for the Newports, had been present at this conversation, but on being brought to give evidence was sworn in only with very great reluctance, and then declared that he knew nothing about it. John was questioned again but while admitting that Cole had spoken to him, neither persuasion nor threats could make him say another word on the subject. John's master was a Mr Wisbey who happened to be a member of the inquest jury, and he now piped up that he had done no more than counsel the boy to tell the truth.

Another juryman, Mr Stevens, now had his say. 'Mr Wisbey, it seems to me that you allow your servants to take a liberty with you which no servant of mine would dare to take with me. When that boy, John Chesham, left this room on the last enquiry, he touched you on the arm, looked up in your face, and smiled. You then said, "Well done, boy, you did it very well."'

The coroner had some stern words to say to Wisbey, since it had been apparent to everyone at the previous hearing that the boy had committed perjury. Wisbey made a poor showing. He first denied that he had spoken to the Newports about it at all, then disclosed he had been to their house to talk to them about the case, but could not recollect anything being said about the boy. Finally he admitted that Thomas Newport had said something to him about arsenic but he had forgotten what. Mr Stevens declared that Wisbey's conduct had been disgraceful. The coroner again turned to John Chesham and asked him who had spoken to him about the evidence he should give. John insisted that he had forgotten, and not a useful word could be drawn from him, so he was dismissed. The complexity of the evidence was such that the inquest was adjourned for several weeks.

On 27 September little Solomon Taylor died, and four days later an inquest was opened at the Cock Inn (since renamed the Old Inn and now a private residence), Manuden, 1 mile from the hovel where he had lived his short life. The room was filled with people and outside the yard and street were thronged with spectators anxious to hear the result. The court heard that the body was emaciated, the child having been unable for some time past to properly absorb nourishment. There was no doubt that he had died as a result of a severe inflammation of the stomach, but the cause was yet to be found. It was necessary to analyse both the child's organs and samples of medicines found in the Chesham house, and Professor Alfred Swaine Taylor was again called in.

The inquest on Joseph and James concluded on 23 October, with Phillip Chesham showing the same reluctance as his brother to tell what he knew.

The coroner regretted that two men who would have been able to give evidence as to the connection between Sarah Chesham and Thomas Newport had been 'most unjustifiably kept out of the way'. He had no doubt at all that the children had been murdered, and the jury agreed, for after a short consultation it returned a verdict of 'wilful murder' against Sarah Chesham. She was duly charged with the murders of her sons and committed to Chelmsford gaol.

The local population had to wait until the end of October to hear the results of the analysis of Solomon Taylor's remains, when it appeared that his long slow demise had been a critical factor in obscuring the primary cause of death. He had wasted away from the failure of his damaged system to absorb nourishment, but what had caused that damage could not be ascertained. Professor Taylor believed that something improper had been given to the child, but nothing found in the Chesham house would have produced the symptoms described. The court concluded that there was insufficient evidence to prove whether the death was one from natural causes or poison.

On 22 December Sarah asked the matron of the gaol to write a letter on her behalf. This bitter little missive was addressed to Thomas Newport, and started by asking him for money which she said he had promised her. In common with many another murderer when found out, Sarah was taking the view that it was someone else's fault, and she had no difficulty in placing all the blame on Newport. 'You deserve to be here more than I do, for you did it

The Old Inn, (formerly the Cock Inn), Manuden. (Author's Collection, by kind permission of Diana and Allan Roe)

and not me,' she wrote, adding, 'It is your money keeps you out of prison . . . Mr Newport you shall support me, for I am suffering for the crime you did – you caused the death of my poor children.' Did Sarah believe that this letter would ever be delivered to Thomas Newport, or was she cunning enough to realise that it could be evidence for the defence? The letter was handed to the prison governor, and was eventually passed to the Home Office.

On 15 January 1847 Thomas Newport, having returned home from a visit to Royston to pay his rent, was met by Inspector Shackell and Superintendent Clarke and arrested on a charge of having feloniously aided and abetted Sarah Chesham in the administration of poison to her two children. The family was said to have offered the police money not to take him away but he was removed to Newport police station, and there left to fret. Sarah's letter was read to him, and while he admitted telling Lydia she should get rid of the child he said that Sarah's allegation was trumped up solely to extort money from him. He was finally released on bail of £800 three weeks later.

On 11 March 1847 Sarah Chesham stood trial, the first indictment being a charge of having murdered her son Joseph. Lord Chief Justice Denman was especially scathing of Mr Hawkes' part in the matter. 'You know nothing about the symptoms of your own knowledge and you had no right to certify that the child died of cholera,' he said sternly, reminding Hawkes that he was well aware of the power of the coroner to order an examination of the body. There was no new evidence. Professor Taylor gave his opinion that Joseph had undoubtedly died from the effects of arsenic.

The defence was simple – there was no proof that Sarah Chesham had actually administered arsenic to the child, and no evidence that arsenic had ever been in her possession. The jury retired and after deliberating for a quarter of an hour returned a verdict of not guilty. The foreman said, 'We have no doubt of the child being poisoned, but we do not see any proof of who administered it.' The jury was challenged by the counsel for the prosecution, and some time elapsed before a second one was empanelled and the indictment for the murder of James proceeded with. The evidence was virtually the same as in the previous case, except that a larger amount of poison had been found in James' stomach. Counsel made an impassioned plea on the prisoner's behalf, stating that witnesses had given evidence that she had always been an affectionate mother and it was therefore impossible that she could have committed such a diabolical act. After a short deliberation she was found not guilty.

Matters did not end there, however. It had been decided, despite the inconclusive inquest verdict on Solomon Taylor, to charge Sarah Chesham with his murder, and Thomas Newport with having 'incited, counselled, hired and commanded her to commit the crime'. Newport was granted bail, but Sarah's trial proceeded. She was reported as being calm, perfectly in control of herself, and almost indifferent to the outcome.

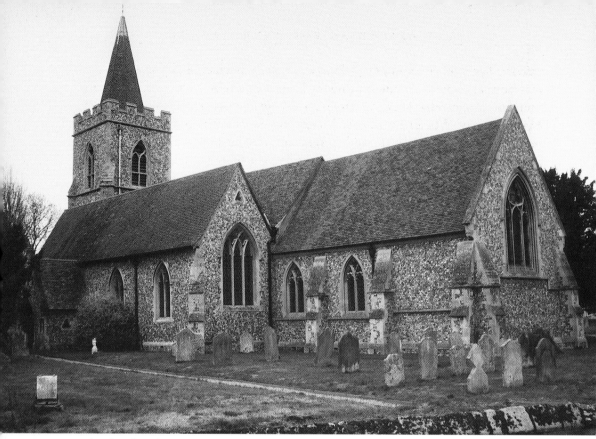

The church and graveyard, Manuden. (Author's Collection)

The case might have seemed strong for there was the evidence of both Lydia and her mother that Sarah had been seen administering poison on three separate occasions, but according to Professor Taylor there was no sign of any poison in the child's body, and it was possible, he admitted, that the death could have been due to natural causes. On hearing this, the prosecutor at once withdrew from the case, and the jury returned a verdict of not guilty. Since the charge against Sarah had failed, that against Newport of aiding and abetting her was not proceeded with.

Newport was not quite out of the woods yet. In July he was charged with the misdemeanour of endeavouring to incite Lydia Taylor to take drugs to produce an abortion. Lydia, who had married and was now Mrs Parker, told the court of Newport's attempts to give her drugs and Mrs Taylor stated that when she had asked him for money before the child was born he had given her four half crowns and said 'It is a bad job and I must try and get rid of it'. In the absence of any direct proof, it was a matter of the Taylors' word against Newport's. The judge directed that the evidence was insufficient to sustain the charge and he was acquitted.

Sarah Chesham returned to the village and her normal ways. It seems that Clavering was a hotbed of gossip on the subject, and Sarah, who may have enjoyed her celebrity and her nickname of 'Sally arsenic', and knew that she was now immune from the law, might have said a little more on the subject than she ought. Her fame certainly spread throughout the county. In 1848 Mary May of Wix in north-east Essex was hanged for poisoning her half brother after insuring him, and it was reported in the press that she had confessed she had been inspired to commit the act by the example of Sarah Chesham. While there were undoubtedly many in Clavering who feared Sarah and kept their children out of her way, there may have been others who came to her either for advice or to enlist her services. The true number of her victims will never be known.

In December 1849 Richard Chesham, who had been complaining of persistent stomach trouble since harvest time, was taken violently ill with symptoms of purging and vomiting. He took to his bed, and was attended to constantly by his wife. Surgeon Hawkes, who seemed to have learned nothing from his previous brush with the Cheshams, was called on 11 February and was unable to form an opinion of what was wrong. He later claimed that he had suggested to Mrs Chesham that her husband's disease was obscure and she should call in further advice, but she declared herself quite satisfied with his services, as no doubt she was. Five weeks later, Richard died. Hawkes performed the post mortem, from which he believed the cause of death to be disease of the lungs, however another doctor attended who noticed clear signs of the effects of an irritant poison. The stomach and its contents were sealed up and sent for analysis. Once again Sarah Chesham's cottage was searched, and one of the items discovered was a bag of rice, which Sarah had used to make milk pudding for her husband. Sarah, who had been unmoved by the search, suddenly became most anxious, and repeatedly asked the police not to remove the rice. Sent to Professor Taylor for analysis, the rice was found to be thoroughly mixed with grains of arsenic.

At the inquest on Richard Chesham, Professor Taylor's evidence was less than conclusive. He had certainly found arsenic in the stomach of the deceased but the quantities were small, and he was unable to say whether it had been the cause of death. He had, however found internal traces of consumption. He thought that the administration of repeated small doses of arsenic to a consumptive would exhaust the energy and could hasten death.

As with little Solomon, the coroner's jury was in the difficult position of having no clear-cut cause of death. Just as it seemed that Sarah Chesham might escape the law again, the coroner made an unusual suggestion. Although it might not be possible to proceed against her on a charge of murdering her husband, he believed the magistrates might consent to hear a charge of attempted murder. With this in mind, depositions were forwarded to the local magistrates, and enquiries were made. Soon, an important new witness came forward. Hannah Phillips was the 48-year-old wife of an agricultural labourer who worked for Thomas Newport. She admitted that she had previously been intimidated into not telling everything she knew, but was now prepared to tell all.

On 2 September 1850 Sarah Chesham was arrested and removed from her cottage to Newport gaol. This time Sarah was less confident, especially when Hannah Phillips gave her evidence before the magistrates. In the last three years Hannah had frequently spoken to Sarah, who had often accused Thomas Newport of poisoning her children. Sarah had said that Newport had given her poison to kill Lydia Taylor and her child, and that she had poisoned the child but not the mother. She had hidden the poison under a slab in Water Lane, and when she came back from Chelmsford gaol she had removed it. Commenting on the ill-treatment of Hannah by her husband William, Sarah declared that she would not live with such a husband, and suggested Hannah make him a poisoned pie, or if she did not know how to season it, she would show her how, it being no sin to bury such a husband.

Even Sarah's family testified against her. Sarah had said that Richard had not eaten any of the rice as he did not like it, but her own mother now stated that she had seen Sarah give Richard rice pudding, indeed she had known of no other person feeding him but Sarah. Her cousin, James Parker, now said that just before the boys died he went with one of them to get arsenic to kill rats and had delivered it to the Chesham house. He had spoken to Richard about their deaths and he had said that they were not poisoned with the arsenic James had bought, which had all been used up. James had mentioned the matter to Thomas Newport who had told him to say nothing about it. Professor Taylor testified that the arsenic had been administered to Richard Chesham in repeated small doses to weaken him. Sarah protested her innocence, but she was committed for trial.

At the Chelmsford spring assizes, Sarah Chesham, described by *The Times* as 'a masculine looking woman', stood trial for the attempted murder of her husband. Her statement which was read to the court now placed the blame for Richard's death on Hawkes, who, she said, had given him something in some medicine to make him sick. As if that wasn't bad enough, she also claimed that Hawkes had neglected him and Richard had been worse when the doctor had not visited. Any inconsistency in these claims was obviously not apparent to her.

Hannah told her full story and another neighbour, Caroline Cole, stated that Sarah had admitted poisoning her sons. The jury spent very little time in returning a verdict of guilty of administering poison with intent to murder. Lord Chief Justice Campbell in pronouncing sentence was not inclined to be lenient. Sarah Chesham was to hang.

The Times wrote with quivering outrage on this and other poisoning cases, describing them as 'wholesale indiscriminate and almost gratuitous assassination'. In many recent cases the scene was a remote village where the inhabitants had 'become perfectly familiarised with the idea of murder by poison.

ago this harvest – She asked me if I had any poison by me that I could give her that she wanted to give it to her Will, that is, her Husband – that he was at home ill at that time and he wanted to go and lie on his own bed and she would not let him – She brought the bed clothes and bed and laid them in the Garden because he should not go to bed – I forgot to tell you that she meant to give the poison to her Husband but she gave it to Emma Chipperfield she told me herself that she had a little and if she had not given it to Emma Chipperfield she meant to give it to her Husband – Five weeks after last Michaelmas she asked me if I had a poison pill to give to her old Man and that if she could get one she would give it him by God – There is a Witness who hears she says but a few weeks ago – There's Sarah Wright Jim Wright and Mrs Mynott told me they heard her say it – There is plenty to know what sort of a woman she is – she is not good – Three different times she asked me for poison – I told my poor Husband, he told me not to say any thing about it, there might be a time to speak about it

The Mark of

Sarah ✝ Chesham

Taken before me at Newport in the County aforesaid the day and year first above mentioned

M Birch Wolfe

Deposition with the mark of Sarah Chesham. (Essex Police Museum)

Certain parties were currently understood to be "poisoners" without incurring thereby any greater disrepute than if they had been poachers or smugglers'.

One aspect of Sarah's career was:

> too remarkable to be passed over, for we doubt whether we will find a parallel in the truths or fictions of even French life. On her first trial a medical witness detailed at some length the deleterious properties of arsenic, and its effects when administered under given conditions and circumstances. The woman, then in peril of her life, stood quietly at the bar, listened, and learnt. No sooner was she discharged than she availed herself of the lesson.

Previously *The Times* said she had poisoned in a 'coarse and unscientific' way, but having become more cunning, she had given her husband small doses, and he expired after six months of slow torture, so very little poison remained to be found in his body.

On 25 March 1851 Sarah Chesham went to the gallows of Springfield gaol, Chelmsford. She was hanged at the same time as Thomas Drory who had strangled his pregnant mistress. A crowd of several thousand had assembled, mainly farming folk, in smock frocks and gaiters, although there were a large number of women of all ages, many of whom had put on their best bonnets for the occasion. Hawkers selling 'true accounts' of the murders and various edibles moved among the crowd. The executioner was William Calcraft, who throughout his career favoured the short drop which killed not by breaking the neck but by slow strangulation. Drory took 4 or 5 minutes to die, but Sarah, being lighter, struggled on for a few more. After an hour the bodies were cut down. Drory's, as was the custom, was buried within the precincts of the prison, but since Sarah had not been found guilty of murder this rule did not apply to her. Phillip Chesham arrived, placed the coffin containing his mother's body on a cart and took it back to Clavering.

When the cart arrived at the Chesham cottage, the coffin was opened and the neighbours arrived to view Sarah's body. The pinioning cords were still round her arms and the marks of the rope could be seen clearly. On 28 March Sarah Chesham was buried in Clavering churchyard without any religious ceremony.

By this time the easy availability of arsenic had become a matter of national concern. There were letters to *The Times* suggesting ways of regulating its sale, and the day before Sarah Chesham was hanged, Lord Carlisle's Bill received its third reading before parliament. The bill proposed that purchasers of arsenic should sign their name in a book, and in certain cases it should only be sold in the presence of a witness. It was also suggested that colouring matter should be added so it did not look like flour or meal. The Bill passed into law on 5 June.

Clavering churchyard where Sarah Chesham and some of her victims are buried. (Author's Collection)

In July Phillip Chesham was seen leaving a shop with a stolen waistcoat hidden under his smock frock. The shopkeeper saw this and followed, and Phillip struck him, but was soon apprehended by a constable. Brought before the court, there were stern words said. The justice commented he would have thought that the dreadful spectacle of his mother's hanging 'would at all events have had the effect of deterring him from a career of crime so soon afterwards, which might eventually lead to the same dreadful consequence'. He was imprisoned with hard labour for six months. Maybe Phillip did take this to heart. He did not end up on the gallows, but settled down to the life of a labourer in Clavering and married. He died there in 1902. Sarah Chesham's other children, who were cared for by grandparents, went on to lead respectable lives.

It would be satisfying to report that fate eventually had a punishment for Thomas Newport, who had undoubtedly, at the very least, conspired to murder Solomon Taylor, but this was not the case. Newport left Clavering and took a farm at nearby Henham, occupying Pledgdon Hall. He married a local girl, fathered a daughter and continued to employ young female servants. He died in 1892, aged seventy-four, and his estate was valued at over £9,200 (about £573,000 today).

5

SWEET LASS OF BUCKHURST HILL, 1867–8

It was 5 a.m. on the morning of Wednesday 24 April 1867, and the thriving market town of Epping, some 17 miles north-east of London, was stirring to life. A young man, who had been wandering hesitantly back and forth outside the local police station, paused, then bracing himself, walked in and approached the duty sergeant. 'I stabbed a young woman last night,' he announced. 'I left her dying in a field.' There was blood on his hands.

The sergeant at once sent to have the officer in charge, Superintendent Patterson, roused from his bed. The young man was searched, but he carried no weapon. He was well dressed and gentlemanly in appearance, but his clothing was dishevelled, as if he had slept in the open overnight. He gave his name as Frederick Alexander Watkins. He was a 23-year-old watchmaker and silversmith, and the son of a London jeweller with a shop on the Strand, the family residing in nearby Covent Garden.

After the usual caution, Superintendent Patterson questioned Watkins, who said that on the previous evening at about 8 p.m. he had attacked his sweetheart, Matilda Griggs, at Buckhurst Hill, a village some 6 miles away. He had struck her on the head with a lead weight, and then stabbed her repeatedly with a knife. Though she was crying out when he ran away, he felt sure that she could not have lived long. It was, he said, a crime of passion. He and Matilda had been keeping company for two years, and a child had been born four months ago. He had offered to marry her many times but she had always refused him. He had become consumed with jealousy, and determined that if he could not have her, no one could. About two days previously, he had decided to kill her.

Watkins, who had related his story quietly, suddenly said he felt sick and asked to be allowed to go out into the yard, saying that he had taken something he ought not to have done, an acid he used in his trade. The Superintendent did not regard this in a serious light, for nothing was done about it at the time. Watkins was at once taken into custody.

Sergeant Fry was sent to Buckhurst Hill, and located the field the prisoner had described. He saw an area of trampled grass where a struggle had obviously taken place, a large pool of blood, a round lead 1lb weight on a string, much dented, and an unusual dagger, five inches in length, which was made from the top of a bayonet set in an ivory umbrella handle. It was still in its leather sheath, but the lower 2 in of the metal protector were missing, and it was heavily stained with blood. The one thing Fry did not find was a body, and this was because Matilda had already been found.

Earlier that morning, a Constable Benns, stationed at Buckhurst Hill, had been walking down the lane from the High Road, when he saw a young woman leaning against a fence, alive, but in obvious distress. Approaching her, he asked what the matter was, and then he saw that her clothing was saturated in blood. At first she was in too much pain to speak, but when she did, she said that her name was Matilda Griggs and she had been stabbed the previous evening and had lain out in the field all night. She was just able to walk with support, so Benns helped her home, where she arrived at about 5 a.m.

Matilda's father, Thomas Griggs, was a well-sinker and general labourer, with a cottage on Princes Road. When he saw the pathetic figure of his injured daughter being helped through the door by a policeman, he almost fainted with the shock, then at once burst into tears. The half-dead girl was laid on her bed, and the local surgeon, Edward Horne, was sent for.

In the meantime, Frederick was revealing more details of his movements the previous night. After stabbing Matilda, he had run away, having sufficient presence of mind not to use the gravel path, but screening himself by running as far as possible across the fields. Reaching the road, he continued his journey in a state of great terror, certain that anyone he encountered would be pointing the finger of suspicion at him. It was nightfall when he arrived at nearby Loughton, and he thought of going to the police station there, but decided not to, the reason he gave being that he thought the police might be asleep and didn't want to wake them. Having walked as far as Epping Forest he lay down for a while under a tree. In his pocket he had a package of oxalic acid, and he took it out and chewed it, but it seemed to boil in his mouth, burning his tongue. He tried a second bite and a third, then thought, 'This is worse than being

Nineteenth-century Essex police constable. (Essex Police Museum)

hanged,' and so went to sleep for about three hours. Arriving at Epping at 2 a.m. he walked about the town until morning, as again, he said that he did not wish to disturb the police so early.

Watkins was astounded when he heard that Matilda was still alive. It must have produced mixed reactions. He was not, as he had thought, a murderer, but on the other hand, a living Matilda might well tell a different tale from the one he had told the police. 'If I had had the presence of mind to have removed the dagger sheath, I would have ended her at once,' he said, whether regretfully or not, we shall never know. Frederick was taken by train to a lock-up in Loughton, where he again complained of feeling unwell. This time a bottle of medicine was brought to him. How much oxalic acid he had consumed was never determined, but he seemed not to suffer any lasting effects.

When Dr Horne arrived at the Griggs' home, and saw the blood-soaked figure of Matilda lying on the bed, his first impression was that he was seeing a corpse. Carefully, he removed the cut and stained clothing. The whole of her back was so bloody that he was unable to see her injuries until he had washed her, and he then found eight wounds, one of them 3in deep. On her left breast were three more stab wounds and there were also two more on her hand where she had tried vainly to defend herself. There were two contusions on her head caused by a blunt object. From the wound in her shoulder he extracted the 2in brass sheath protector of the dagger. It had penetrated her lung, and she was coughing up blood, however the plugging of the wound by the sheath had partly contributed to her survival. Some of the wounds had clearly been inflicted by the knife while still in its sheath, and when the brass part had broken away, by the blade itself. Two of the wounds he considered extremely dangerous.

Horne did the best he could, and Matilda survived the night, but on Thursday, he gave a certificate that her condition had declined to the extent that he did not believe she would live. Not only was there considerable loss of blood, but the hours of lying in the wet grass had caused acute inflammation of the lungs. A special bench of magistrates was therefore convened at Waltham Abbey to take the girl's dying deposition. Two magistrates, Mr Williams and Mr Edenborough, hurried to the house, and Frederick Watkins was also brought there. After he had been questioned, Matilda was raised up in the bed and told her story.

Matilda Griggs was born on 3 April 1851, the oldest child of Thomas and Sarah Griggs. Since the arrival of the railways in 1856, the small rural village of Buckhurst Hill had undergone a phase of development, and freeholds were being sold for building land. One of these was purchased by Frederick's father, who was building up a portfolio of property investments to fund his retirement. Part of the land was being used for a brick-making venture, which Frederick was supervising. When Matilda met Frederick, he was twenty-one,

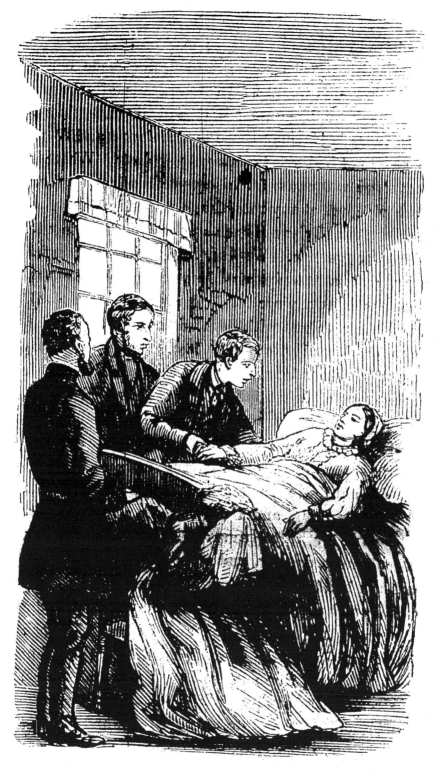

A contemporary artist's impression of Matilda Griggs being interviewed.
(Illustrated Police News)

and Matilda just fourteen, a sturdy and attractive country girl with a healthy outdoor complexion. Frederick had seduced his country lass, and thereafter Matilda always claimed to be a year older than she actually was, perhaps to protect him, for she was pregnant at fourteen, and a mother at fifteen.

Frederick continued to visit Matilda and their daughter Jessie three or four times a week, travelling by rail to Buckhurst Hill, and he paid her £2 10s a week (about £115 today) towards the child's upkeep, for she had no trade or income of her own. Her parents seemed not to object to this arrangement, for, apart from the useful income, they clearly hoped that in due course, when Matilda was sixteen, Frederick would marry her. Such a liaison would have been greatly to Matilda's advantage, for there was a wide gulf in both wealth and social position between the couple.

As a well-dressed young jeweller Frederick had felt in some danger from thieves, particularly the garrotters who then infested Covent Garden, for he carried with him a dagger he had made himself by setting a bayonet into an ivory handle, the leather sheath having a fine brass protector.

As Matilda's sixteenth birthday approached, so the anxious Griggs grandparents began to drop hints about marriage. Both Matilda and her mother were of the belief that the couple were actually engaged, and a dress had been made for the wedding, but Frederick was curiously reluctant to name a date. The couple remained on friendly terms, but when in early April Thomas Griggs tackled Frederick outright on the subject of marriage the young man became suddenly very distracted and was unable to frame a coherent reply.

On the evening of 23 April Frederick had come up from London on the train and called on Matilda. She was going up to a new freehold to see a neighbour, and he asked to walk with her, but having reached the neighbour's house, he suggested they walk on. Frederick suddenly tried to start a quarrel with Matilda, accusing her of 'speaking to' other men, something she at once denied. They walked a little further and he persuaded her to go into the field over some palings. Trustingly, she accompanied him. There he drew from his pocket the lead weight on a string and struck her over the head with it several times until the string broke. Matilda fell to her knees begging for mercy. Frederick then rained blows upon her with his dagger, in his agitation forgetting to take the weapon out of its sheath.

Matilda collapsed, her blood staining the grass. She was aware of her lover leaning over her to see if she was still breathing. 'Freddy! Freddy!' she cried, but he was already running away. There she lay for a long time, unable to move, drifting in and out of consciousness. After a time she heard the village clock striking 10 p.m. She tried to get up but could not, but eventually she managed to crawl across the grass through a fence into the next field. Two calves, the only witnesses to the incident, followed her. Exhausted by the effort, she lay still. The weather that April had been unusually cold, and as the night wore on, the temperature dropped, and it began to rain heavily. As

A contemporary artist's impression of the attack on Matilda Griggs. (Illustrated Police News)

Matilda lay shivering, the calves ambled forward and lay, one on either side of her, their body heat keeping her warm. Hours passed, and after another desperate attempt, she managed to get to her feet and head in the direction of home, but weak from loss of blood, had to support herself against a fence, where, some eight hours after the event, she was found.

Frederick listened quietly to Matilda's story, and when she had finished, he seemed moved by her condition and asked if he might shake hands with her. The magistrates agreed, and he went over to the bed and kissed her and shook her hand. 'Goodbye, Tilly, goodbye,' he said, and burst into tears. She made no reply.

Sergeant Fry turned to the prisoner. 'The charge against you is cutting and wounding with intent to murder,' he said.

'That is quite right,' said Watkins. 'I suppose if she dies I shall be hanged.' Looking down at his muddy and blood-spattered boots he added, 'Jack Ketch [a common name for the public hangman after a notorious seventeenth-century executioner] will not get much for my boots before they are cleaned.' He was led away through the large crowd that had gathered outside Matilda's house and was removed to Ilford gaol by train. On the way he had so far recovered his composure that on seeing a lady he knew on a platform, he waved his handcuffed hands at her. In the gaol the warders removed his handkerchief, and on enquiring why, he was told that it was for fear he should hang himself. 'I would rather leave that to others,' he observed dryly.

Matilda lingered on in a perilous state, with every expectation that each day would be her last, but to the great surprise of her doctor, her condition began to improve. Mrs Jane Watkins, Frederick's mother, came to see her on the Saturday, and was permitted to stay with her all night. Her offer to remain and nurse Matilda day and night was not accepted.

Sunday being a day of rest, when day trips were a popular pastime, crowds of people arrived at Buckhurst Hill by train to see the scene of the crime. Only relatives were allowed in to see the patient, but the rest, who were strangers, stood outside the house asking to see Matilda and some went to examine the bloody field, and the fence where Matilda had leaned, cutting away pieces of bloodstained wood with their pocket knives as souvenirs. The local press deplored the sightseers and pointedly suggested that Matilda's condition had become worse as a result of the crowds, but had improved after they left. The medical profession had already taken quite an interest in Matilda, as she had been able to get up and walk after injuries that would have proved fatal to another person, something her doctor attributed to 'the extraordinary power of endurance of her wonderfully strong constitution'.

On 30 April Frederick Watkins was charged with cutting and wounding Matilda Griggs with intent to murder her. The defendant, described in the press as an intelligent-looking young man with a fair complexion and regular features, 5ft 8in in height, was defended by Mr Abrams, a solicitor from Bow Street. The only witness examined was Dr Horne, who testified to the wounds he had found on Matilda's body, and was able to report that she was progressing very favourably, and if there was no relapse, would shortly be able to attend court to give evidence.

Frederick's application for bail was refused and he was remanded in custody. His brother visited him in gaol, and despite the ignominy of prison garb, found Frederick in strangely high spirits, asking what he thought of the new 'uniform'.

On 4 May Mrs Jane Watkins came to see Matilda again. Quite what was said on that occasion was never revealed, but subsequent events suggest that the visit was not prompted by sympathy for the gravely injured young woman.

On Tuesday 14 May Frederick Watkins was again brought before the magistrates at Waltham Abbey. The quiet, picturesque little town was thrown into great excitement by the prospect of Matilda's appearance, and the demand for space in the magistrates' court was such that it was decided at the last minute to hold the hearing in the county court. Watkins had to be walked down the street to the courthouse, while the police tried to hold back crowds who ran along the road beside him to get a good look. Matilda, wearing her

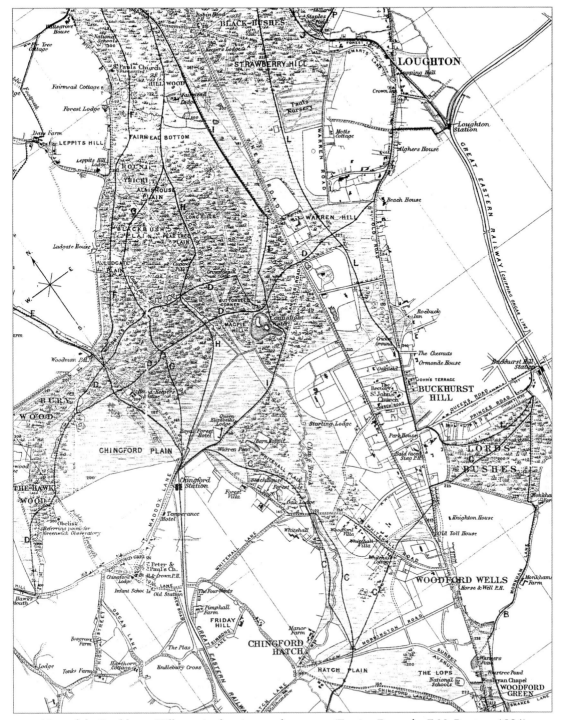

Map of the Buckhurst Hill area in the nineteenth century. (Epping Forest by E.N. Buxton, 1884)

best dress and bonnet, was brought to the court by her parents, with Dr Horne in attendance. She was obviously still very weak, and was allowed to be seated. Her deposition was read to her, and she was able to confirm its accuracy in a faint voice, but was soon overcome by the effort, and sank back in her chair. Dr Horne assisted her from the court.

By now, a number of things had become clear. Frederick's tale about his fit of jealousy, and his many entreaties to Matilda to marry him, which he had told when he thought she was dead, was looking a little unconvincing. It was known that his family had been violently opposed to any question of marriage beneath his class, and had threatened that if he did marry Matilda, he would never darken their doors again. Far from being committed to the capture of his lovely bride, he had during the previous two years ashamedly kept the liaison a secret from his well-to-do friends. At the time of the stabbing, therefore, Frederick had been under pressure from Matilda's parents to regularise the relationship, and under pressure from his own parents to do nothing of the sort.

Mr Abrams, aware that the 'crime of passion' defence might not hold water, took the only course that seemed open to him. On Matilda's return to court he questioned her closely, with a view to showing that the prisoner had on the night in question and on previous occasions shown symptoms of high excitement suggestive of insanity. Matilda loyally denied that she had ever noticed anything in her Frederick's behaviour to produce any feeling other than that of confidence and affection. Abrams pressed her closer on the question, and might have wished that he had not, for she then recollected that the only time Frederick had seemed to be wandering in his mind was the time six weeks ago when her father had called attention to the necessity of their getting married. The prisoner was duly committed for trial at the Old Bailey, there being two alternative indictments, that of attempted murder and a lesser one of wounding with intent to do grievous bodily harm.

When the case came up before Mr Justice Wiles on 13 June 1867 matters took a sudden and unexpected turn. Before the trial could commence, Mr Straight, on behalf of the prosecution, rose and made an application for the trial to be postponed to the next session. His reason was that Matilda Griggs, the prosecutrix and material witness, was nowhere to be found. He had been informed that she had been got out of the way by the prisoner's mother in order to prevent her giving evidence. Matilda, it seemed, had been kidnapped.

Mr Ribton, counsel for the defence, opposed the application. He knew nothing of the reasons for Matilda not being present, but he did not think her evidence would carry the case further than it would go without her. The prisoner's own statements had made the case as clear as it could be without the evidence of the prosecutrix and the only question for the jury was which count of the indictment applied. Mr Justice Wiles considered the unusual position, and said he did not think it would be satisfactory to try the case without Matilda's evidence, and agreed to the postponement.

When the trial re-opened on 10 July before Mr Baron Bramwell, Matilda was still missing, but it had by now been established that she had not been kidnapped, but had gone away of her own free will, albeit at the persuasion of and with the financial assistance of Frederick's parents. By doing so, she naïvely believed that she would enable Frederick to go free, for despite everything, she still loved him and wanted to be his wife. That much was clear from the letter she addressed to him from Berlin.

My Dear Fred

I hope you dont [sic] think it ankind [sic] at my staying away from the trial it for your good I do so and I am waiting anxiously in the hope of hearing that you are free and I am looking for the time when we shall be united and happy once again for without you I cannot be happy allthough [sic] I am quite well in body all the past is forgot.
From your true own
tilley [sic] Griggs

This note come [sic] enclosed to a friend in London who will cause it to be given to you T.G.

This time the trial proceeded, and Sarah Griggs confirmed that her daughter had gone away with Mrs Watkins and she had not seen her since and did not know where she was. The remaining witnesses duly gave evidence, but the best evidence of all was that of Matilda, for although she was not present, there was the deposition she had made when she thought herself to be dying and which was put before the court.

Mr Straight for the prosecution made his final address to the jury. He asked them not to be led astray by his learned friend who would try and convince them that the prisoner inflicted the injuries with the intention merely of doing bodily harm. The injuries spoke for themselves, for it must surely follow that anyone who inflicted such serious multiple wounds upon a defenceless person must have done so with the intention of killing.

Mr Ribton for the defence had a difficult task, for his client was undoubtedly guilty of causing grievous bodily harm to a young woman who was extremely fortunate to survive his attack. Ribton's aim, however was not so much to try and convince the jury that his client had no intention of killing Matilda when he hit her on the head with a lead weight and stabbed her thirteen times, but to convince them that the lesser charge was a preferable one. Ribton knew his juries well. With a little careful leading they would often give prisoners the benefit of the doubt, and they also responded well to being flattered that they had the power of mercy in their hands. Emphasising that Frederick had struck Matilda with a sheathed dagger, he said that there could have been no motive to kill at the time of the attack, which had taken place in a moment of wild excitement fuelled by jealousy. Having extracted as much sympathy for his client as he could, he suggested to the jury that they would find it a far more agreeable duty to find the unhappy man guilty on the second count than on the graver and more serious offence.

Mr Baron Bramwell made it clear to the jury that the absence of the prosecutrix who very likely would pardon her lover and still be willing to take him for better or worse could not in the least benefit him. The trial, he reminded them, was instituted on public grounds in order that other women might not be similarly ill treated and injured. He charged them to consider the facts of the case and in particular, the injuries sustained, to say whether the prisoner was guilty of wounding with intent to kill, or whether he merely attacked her with the intention of inflicting grievous bodily harm.

The jurymen deliberated, and it seemed that their hearts had been touched, for after a brief discussion they found Frederick Watkins guilty only of unlawful wounding with intent to do grievous bodily harm.

Mr Bramwell, who clearly disapproved of the verdict, growled that he could hardly imagine a worse crime than that of which the prisoner had been found guilty. He had considered imposing the maximum penalty the law would allow, but on further consultation, had decided to sentence the prisoner to penal servitude for twenty years.

Frederick was led away to begin his sentence, and Matilda, disappointed by the outcome, eventually returned home to Buckhurst Hill, under the impression that she could settle down to her old, quiet life. This was not to be.

The law as it stood required Matilda to attend court to prosecute Frederick Watkins, and her failure to do so rendered her liable to a fine of £40, which was exactly £40 more than she owned in the world. On Christmas Eve 1867 the Sheriff's officers went to see her, and having established that she was unable to pay the debt, she was arrested and taken to Essex County gaol. Matilda lay in prison until 18 January when she was brought before the County Court, where she was obliged to present her petition to be adjudicated bankrupt. She looked healthy, and was smartly dressed. On being questioned by the Registrar, she confirmed that she had not appeared to prosecute as she thought that without her evidence, Frederick would not be convicted. The plan had been for her to stay with his parents until he was freed and then marry him. Even now, she said she was unable to fathom the reasons for his attack. She had never given Frederick any cause for jealousy or refused to be his wife, and the reports which said she had done so were untrue. As for the debt, she was unable to pay it, as she had no trade and her father was very poor.

Captain McGorrey the prison governor, who was obviously sympathetic to her plight, commented that it was a sad case, but his plea was in vain. The Registrar said that as she had no trade, the law stated that she had to remain in gaol for at least two months before her petition could be heard. The next hearing in mid-February was too early. Matilda was therefore sent back to gaol with no prospect of her case being heard until March.

There she would have remained, but the newspapers had scented a tale to tug at the emotions, and on 21 January the *Daily Telegraph* published an impassioned plea for mercy for the 'profusely-perforated damsel'. 'It is clear,' it stated, 'that the hearts and brains of our great lawyers never provided for the contingency of a Matilda Griggs. Where is the father of Watkins the watchmaker, that he does not if necessary sell his last mainspring and escapement and buy this free-hearted girl out of prison?' The newspaper's exhortation to its readers to 'club up the money' had immediate effect, and letters poured in, including one from the art historian John Ruskin with a cheque for £40. The donations eventually totalled £110. A telegram was at once sent to the Governor, who sent a Sheriff's officer with the demand, and he duly returned with the money. On 22 January Matilda was on the 3.15 p.m. train home.

What eventually became of young Watkins we do not know. Perhaps, on his release from prison, his doting parents sent him abroad. Matilda did have her Frederick after all, as she married Frederick Elliott, a tailor, took up the trade of tailoress and settled in Leytonstone, where their three children were born. One can only hope that their lives were pleasant and unexciting.

6

THE MAN AT WITHAM STATION, 1893–1901

Nearly 150 years after the shooting of Daniel Brett the inhabitants of Colchester were to be shocked by a remarkable murder which sparked off a worldwide manhunt, and stimulated an advance in forensic science.

Alfred Welch was a tailor and outfitter whose premises occupied the corner of Short Wyre Street and St Botolph's Street. Born in Hertfordshire in about 1829, at the age of twenty-five he had married Emma Clarke, one year his junior. The family had spent some time in London before settling in Colchester. In 1881 there were six children, two sons and four daughters, the family residing at 16 Queen Street, next door to a theatre. By 1893 Alfred Welch was regarded as something in the community. A prominent Freemason and Past Master of the Angel Lodge, a member of the cyclists' club, a Swedenborgian by religion, a devotee of culture who was reputed to be able to converse on any subject, he had for many years been an art collector and was well known in the local galleries. No one, it seemed, had a bad word to say about Alfred Welch.

At 9.40 p.m. on Friday 8 December 1893 PC George Alexander, on his regular beat in central Colchester, saw smoke coming from the roof at the back of Welch's premises. On further investigation, he saw that the upper storey was ablaze. The fire brigade was summoned and the Colchester volunteer fire fighters soon arrived, followed by the Essex and Suffolk brigade, the head constable and fire master Mr Coombs, a police inspector, the waterworks superintendent, the borough surveyor, an alderman, members of the Corporation and a crowd of interested spectators.

Volunteer fireman Henry Rice broke the door down and entered the premises. It was dark, so he lit the gas, not, perhaps the wisest of moves, but luckily he came to no harm. Rushing up to the first-floor landing he found the upper stairs and the cupboard underneath them well alight, a heap of burning material suggesting that this was where the fire had begun.

The occupants of adjoining premises were evacuated and six jets of water played on the flames, which were being fanned by a stiff south-westerly breeze. It took several hours to bring it under control. One of the volunteer firemen was 37-year-old Henry

Alfred Welch. (Essex Telegraph)

Sizzey, who by day was a foreman at Welch's shop. Asked where Welch was likely to be, he told Coombs that he would probably be at his club. Someone was quickly dispatched to the club to inform Welch of the fire, but he wasn't there, neither was he at home or visiting friends. As time wore on and he did not make an appearance, it seemed increasingly likely that he might not have left the shop after all. It was 1 a.m. before it was possible to search the premises. The roof of the building had been destroyed, as well as the upper storey which housed the cutting room and stores. The floors below, which comprised the offices and the shop, were badly damaged by water. On the first-floor landing, at the bottom of the second staircase, was found what everyone had most feared – the charred remains of a human body. It had not been there when Rice had first entered, but the fact that it was lying on a heap of debris suggested it had fallen down the staircase with the collapse of the upper floor.

Essex police constable, c. 1910. (Essex Police Museum)

Sizzey became hysterical. 'If there's one then there are two!' he is said to have exclaimed, though he could never afterwards recollect his words or why he had spoken them. He ran forward and took hold of the blackened head of the corpse. As he did so part of the skull crumbled, his thumb going through it into the brain. 'Blatch murdered my poor master!' he said, again and again. It was with some difficulty that he was removed from the scene. Outside in the street he went on shouting 'He is a murderer! He is a murderer!' A local doctor, Jonathan Becker, was called and saw the body, then it was carefully carried to what had been Welch's office. Although it was unrecognisable there was little doubt that it was Welch. The keys of the deed box had lain beside the body, and encircling it was the remains of a double truss which Welch was known to have worn. There was another detail about the body which greatly concerned the police. A charred rope was wound around its neck, leading to the initial belief that Welch had committed suicide. No one who knew the dead man gave much credence to this idea, but it directed the course of investigations for the vital period of time soon after the discovery of the body.

Henry Sizzey. (Colchester Gazette)

The job of sifting the debris would be enormous and could not commence until the body was removed, so the building, still with the body in position, was locked up, and a coroner's inquiry convened at the Town Hall on Saturday afternoon, the day after the fire, to enable formal identification. The events had naturally caused a great deal of excitement in the area. With the weather being exceptionally fine for the time of year, many people both in the town and from outlying areas took the opportunity that weekend for an outing to see the burnt-out shop, and large crowds milled around the centre of Colchester.

It was, even for an inquest, an unusually solemn occasion, since Welch had been known personally to Mr Church, the coroner, and most of the jury, and was greatly liked and respected. The jury walked to the gutted premises making their way through the throngs of sightseers. The appearance of the body must have been a shock to even the strongest stomach. The head, which was bent down to the left, was a featureless blackened ball, with hardly anything to indicate that it had ever been a human head. The torso was similarly charred, only the exposed rib bones showing what had been the man's chest. The legs had been burned away up to the thighs which were jagged stumps, and the hands and forearms were also gone. The right upper arm sloped downwards, but the left, which was the only part of the body not charred, was extended at right angles to the body, an odd position for a supposedly hanged man. The jury examined the area where the body had been found and then trooped back to the Town Hall.

The coroner then proceeded to take the evidence. First to be questioned was Henry Sizzey who appeared dressed in his fireman's uniform. Sizzey had been employed by Welch for some thirteen to fourteen years. He was closely questioned about Welch's state of mind and whether he would be likely to take his own life, and was adamant that his employer would never do such a thing. He also revealed that the deed box, which should have contained the shop takings since the last banking on Tuesday 5th, and a cash float, was empty. On the morning of the fire, Sizzey had been at the shop as usual and Welch had told him he was going to London that day. Sizzey managed the shop in Welch's absence, so when Welch returned at 7.30 p.m. he questioned Sizzey about how the day had gone. Welch, said Sizzey, had then turned to him and said 'Whom do you think I saw just now? I saw that unfortunate fellow George'. 'George' was actually Arthur Blatch, a 35-year-old Colchester man, who two years previously had been employed by Welch as a porter. Blatch had repeatedly taken time off work claiming illness, but it had later been discovered that he was lying, and his employment had ceased. He had then left Colchester, although his wife still lived at 21 Chapel Street. That evening Welch had been approached by Blatch who had been lurking in the shadows by the theatre. Blatch told Welch he needed to speak to him as 'something terrible' had happened (or was about to happen, Sizzey could not recall which). Welch invited him to come to the shop, but Blatch demurred, saying he didn't want to see Sizzey. Why he should say this, Sizzey didn't know, as he believed that they had parted on friendly terms. Welch had suggested to Blatch that he come after closing time at 8 p.m., but was determined to give him no more than five minutes of his time. He shared Sizzey's opinion that Blatch probably wanted to borrow money, and had no intention of giving him any. At a few minutes to eight, the blinds were drawn, the shop locked up and the employees departed. Welch, who had a bunch of keys which gave him access to his office and the upper storerooms, had remained alone on the premises.

After Dr Becker had given his evidence the jury indicated by a show of hands that they were satisfied as to the identity of the deceased, and the court was adjourned. It was determined that a policeman should be

Arthur Blatch. (Essex Country Standard)

sent to London to try and find Blatch, with the intention of serving a summons on him to appear at the adjourned inquest. There was one clue as to his whereabouts. The previous February, in Witham, Blatch had been found ill and exhausted on the street by a postman called George Robjent, who had taken him home and given him food. The two men seemed to have struck up a friendship, and Blatch later wrote a letter to Robjent. The address he gave was 94 Great Titchfield Street, London. Sergeant Charles Alexander (probably the brother of the constable who had found the fire) was duly dispatched to that address, which was a lodging house. He found that Blatch and a young woman had been living there as husband and wife, but the landlady, Mrs Lincoln, said the couple had left, removing all their belongings over a month previously. Alexander made some further fruitless enquiries and soon afterwards returned to Colchester.

On the Sunday afternoon Dr Becker together with Dr Maybury, a police medical attendant, commenced examination of the body, which still lay in the premises. They had scarcely done so for an hour when the process was stopped by order of the coroner. Two local doctors, Cook and Laver, had written to the coroner, urging him that the matter was serious enough for a Home Office expert to be summoned. On Monday Head Constable Goody went to London to make the arrangements, and notification was made by telegram that Metropolitan Police Surgeon Dr Thomas Bond would arrive on Tuesday. A man of considerable experience in post mortem examinations, Bond had carried out the examination of the mutilated corpse of Mary Jane Kelly, victim of Jack the Ripper, in 1888.

Exterior of Welch's shop after the fire. (Colchester Gazette)

One fact had already emerged. The rope found on the deceased was wound around his neck three or four times, a most unlikely circumstance if he had hanged himself. Public opinion was coming firmly round to the idea that Welch had been murdered, especially as it had been confirmed that £100 in cash was missing. Fresh rumours flowed. The behaviour of Sizzey at the scene seemed highly suspicious – could he have murdered his employer and concocted the story about the mysterious appointment? Had his seizing of the charred head been an attempt to destroy evidence? On 12 December the *Essex Telegraph* was to comment that if Blatch really had been in Colchester on the previous Friday, no one seemed to have seen him.

Dr Bond arrived on the 10.42 a.m. train from London and, accompanied by the Head Constable, at once proceeded to the premises, where, some four days after his death, the body of Alfred Welch still lay, the cause of death still undetermined. There, Bond was joined by Becker and Maybury. They rolled up their sleeves and the post mortem resumed, an interested crowd having gathered outside, trying to peer through the windows. Examining the ruined head, Bond found that on the upper back part of the skull on the right-hand side, there was an extensive fracture, and just over the right ear, brain matter was protruding. Directly under the bone was a large amount of dark red putty-like matter, an inch thick, which he later confirmed was dried blood. Bond also examined a deep groove around the neck about 1½in wide, and Becker showed him the rope which he had removed from the corpse. He concluded that the injuries to the skull had obviously been inflicted on a living man and were more than sufficient to cause his death. Moreover, they could not have been caused by a fall down stairs – some heavy blunt implement had been used, probably by an assailant standing behind him. There was no fracture of the neck and no sign of suffocation. Bond departed from Colchester by the 12.33 p.m. train. Later that day the news was released that Welch had indeed been murdered, and the rope had been placed around his neck after death.

Meanwhile, evidence was beginning to flow in to support Sizzey's story. Two of his fellow employees had heard Welch's comments about meeting Blatch, and several people were claiming to have seen him in Colchester. Many of these stories turned out to be a case of mistaken identity and much time was wasted, but a bootmaker called Went, who had known Blatch personally, confirmed that he had seen him lurking by the theatre at about 7.50 p.m. on the Friday. It was fortunate for Sizzey that after leaving the shop on the night of the murder he had met with and spoken to a number of other volunteer firemen, such that his movements could easily be checked. He was soon cleared of all suspicion, which now firmly pointed at the missing Arthur Blatch.

The funeral, which was held on 15 December, was a substantial affair, the procession included large contingents of local tradesmen, cyclists and Freemasons. The blinds were drawn all along Wyre Street at noon and trading was suspended for two hours. The horse-drawn funeral car was brought to

Colchester High Street, early twentieth century. (Author's Collection)

the door of the premises and the coffined remains removed. It then proceeded along Wyre Street to Queen Street where the chief mourners joined the procession. The cortège then passed slowly by the blackened premises, and on to St Botolph's Church, the streets deeply lined with solemn spectators.

On the same day Inspector Summons and Sergeant Alexander headed back to London to try and find Arthur Blatch, who was now wanted for murder. The policemen again spoke to Mrs Lincoln who said that 'Mr and Mrs Blatch' had lodged with her for twelve weeks until the previous June. They had been away during the summer, and returned at the end of October, departing finally around 4 November. Blatch had changed his profession since leaving Welch's having hired a camera and set himself up as an itinerant photographer, but the enterprise was only intermittently successful as the main part of his business was done among the summer holiday crowds at the seaside.

Someone with a rather more intimate knowledge of Arthur Blatch was Sarah Elizabeth Rash (usually referred to as Elizabeth Sarah) the 22-year-old daughter of a bricklayer, who had known him for four years. Initially unaware that he was a married man, this discovery seemed not to have prevented the blossoming of a close relationship. She had been working as a servant to Mr Briggs, a dentist of Head Street, during which time it was said that she had performed some act of kindness to Blatch, the nature of which was never revealed. Shortly after Blatch left Welch's employment Briggs was due to go on holiday and Miss Rash was asked to keep house in his absence. Unknown to Briggs, Blatch had arranged to stay with Elizabeth during that time, but at the last moment Briggs had changed his mind and arranged to have her boarded out while he was away. Blatch and his lady friend went instead to the Berechurch Arms (now the Huntsmans Tavern), Shrub End, just outside Colchester, asking to be lodged in separate rooms. During the time they stayed there they seemed anxious to avoid meeting up with other people. After a week Blatch confided in the landlady that he and Miss Rash had just been married by special licence. On departing, Elizabeth retrieved her luggage from Mr Briggs' house and went at once to London where she and Blatch were united. This was undoubtedly the woman with whom Blatch had been living at Great Titchfield Street. The police were most anxious to interview her.

Police notices were circulated with descriptions of the couple. Blatch was 5ft 8in, thin, with a pale complexion, while his hair, moustache and eyes were dark. Stooping slightly, he walked with short, quick steps, and was known to have a bad back. Elizabeth Rash was of medium height, with a stout build, fresh complexion, light hair and blue eyes, but with a rather large nose and a small scar on the back of her hand. She was said to suffer from a weak heart and have an excitable nature.

Only one person in Colchester was resolutely determined that Arthur Blatch was innocent and that was his wife, Emma, who was some four or five years his senior. The couple had married in 1876 and had no children. She told a

PRESSING AND IMPORTANT.

SUSPECTED

MURDER,
ROBBERY & ARSON.

On the Evening of FRIDAY, the 8th inst., the Shop and Premises of a Tradesman in this Borough were found to be on fire, and his charred body was subsequently recovered from the ruins. A safe upon the premises was robbed of nearly £100.

A man named ARTHUR BLATCH, formerly in the employ of the deceased as Porter, is said to have been the last person in his company that Evening at the Shop, and it is highly important that his whereabouts should be discovered if possible.

POLICE OFFICERS are requested to make every possible enquiry for him, and if found, to detain him, or cause observation to be kept upon him until an officer can be sent to identify.

BLATCH has been travelling the Country, taking Cheap Photographs with a small Camera belonging to the NATIONAL PHOTO Co., LONDON, and he recently visited the South Coast Watering Places. It is not known what he is now doing. He is generally accompanied by a woman named RASH whose photo is also attached.

3 POSTAL ORDERS for £1 each were stolen, numbered & 572,693, 572,695, 572,696; PLEASE WARN POST OFFICES.

A Gent's Gold Hunting Geneva Lever Watch, Independent centre seconds, No. 9728, 3 Key-holes at back, white dial, in wear 15 years, was also stolen. Please give information to pawnbrokers and others.

ARTHUR BLATCH
Age about 18 or 16,
Height about 6ft. 6i.
Complexion—pale,
Eyes—dark,
Hair—dark,
Moustache—dark,
Face thin, rather high cheek bones
Stoops slightly,
Thin build, Narrow Chest,
Walks with short quick steps and has suffered from an affection of the spine.
Has been in hospital and may go to one again.

ELIZABETH RASH
Age 24,
Solid—stout,
Height—medium,
Complexi n—dark,
Eyis—blue,
Hair—light,
Nose rather large,
Scar about the size of a half-penny on back of hand.
Suffers from a weak heart and is of an excitable nature.

Information to be sent to
R. O. COOMBS,
Chief Constable.

Police Office,
Colchester,
13th December, 1893.

WILES & SON, "TRINITY PRINTING WORKS" TRINITY STREET, COLCHESTER

The wanted poster for Blatch and Rash. (Essex Telegraph)

reporter that her husband had once been a footman in the home of a gentleman in London and had come to Colchester with excellent testimonials. He had then been appointed keeper of the public recreation ground, but was obliged to give this up due to an inability to do hard manual work. He had left Colchester two years ago to look for a better position in London, and although he had written to her from there, she had not heard from him or had a penny maintenance since April, a circumstance she attributed to his having been ill. She had been obliged to support herself by working as a cleaner and taking in lodgers. She knew about Blatch's visit to the Berechurch Arms, and had gone there and spoken to the landlady. She had been assured that her husband and Miss Rash had occupied separate rooms. 'A man may have a friend without there being anything wrong,' she told the *Essex Telegraph*. She was also adamant that the story of Blatch having been in Colchester asking to see Mr Welch on the fatal night was a complete invention. The fact that there were three witnesses to Welch's comments would not shake her from this point of view.

Police efforts to find Blatch and his companion were concentrated in London. Summons and Alexander were anxious to discover from Mrs Lincoln how the missing couple had departed her premises. They visited her on 16 December and Summons saw her again four days later. After some initial uncertainty she said that she believed they had left in a four-wheeled cab. Placards were placed at all the cab stands in case anyone recalled where the couple had gone. A careful watch was also kept at all ports.

Gradually it became possible to piece together some of Blatch's movements. His postman friend Robjent had last seen him at Witham on 11 November. Blatch said that he had been in Plymouth during the summer with his camera, but intended to head back to Colchester and buy some fancy goods ready for the Christmas season. Blatch must have remained in Essex, for on 28 November he was seen by a Mrs Cardy of Maldon Road, Colchester, who had known him well. He was in need of money and was 'on the cadge'. More interestingly, the wide circulation of photographs of the missing man had caused a number of people to realise that they had seen him within hours of the murder.

Four miles from the centre of Colchester was a public house called the Stanway Swan. The landlord, Henry Ollard, had closed up the premises as usual at 10 p.m. on the night of 8 December. About forty-five minutes later there was a knock at the door. The stranger standing outside, who seemed to be out of breath, said that he had walked there from Colchester that night. Declining to enter, he asked for a bottle of brandy and a glass of ale. The man, who had a thin face and pale complexion, was wearing a long coat and a black and white check cap, and carried a willow basket and a long canvas case. Soon after he had drunk the ale and pocketed the brandy bottle the stranger departed, leaving Ollard with the strong impression that he wished to avoid being seen.

Just over an hour later the same man was seen by a Constable Isom on the way to Kelveden railway station, some 6 miles from the Stanway Swan, but he did not take a train there, and walked on, hoping to get the mail train at Witham, another 4 miles along the road.

At approximately 2.20 a.m. on 9 December, with the rain falling fast, a stranger walked into Witham station asking when the mail train departed and was distressed to find that it had left some seven or eight minutes before and there would not be another train for several hours. He was anxious to get to London as quickly as possible and made enquiries about getting someone to drive him to another station where he might get a train, stating that he hardly cared how much he paid. No driver was forthcoming, and the man was obliged to remain at Witham. He was carrying a wicker basket and a canvas case and the station staff assumed that he was a fisherman. Restless and anxious at first, he had eventually settled down. When he removed his long coat, which was dripping with rainwater, the pockets bulged and clinked with money. He revealed that he had important business to do in London, and a large amount of money to pay out. He carried no food, and was very hungry. One of the porters, William Allaby, gave him food and tea and the stranger gave him a cigar from a supply he kept in his pocket. The claim to be carrying a lot of money was not mere boasting – Allaby later saw the stranger counting some coins, which included a respectable number of sovereigns and half sovereigns. More than five hours later the next train arrived. It was 7.48 a.m. when the stranger finally departed. When the police heard this story they had no doubt that Ollard, Isom and the staff at Witham station had all seen Arthur Blatch.

Inspector Summons was becoming increasingly certain that Mrs Lincoln was not telling all she knew. He interviewed her a total of seven times, but it wasn't until his visit on 23 December that she finally decided to tell the uncomfortable truth.

According to 61-year-old Mrs Lincoln, the couple she knew as Mr and Mrs Blatch had returned to London after working away for the summer, but on 23 October 1893 Blatch had taken his camera and gone to find work. While he was away the rent, which was 7s a week, was unpaid, and she had asked Elizabeth, who had no income, when her 'husband' would be returning. Elizabeth claimed that Blatch had been ill but would be returning soon. Mrs Lincoln next saw him late on the morning of 9 December, when he appeared with the rent money in his hand. Blatch had a favour to ask. He said he had tried to mortgage some property and his 'friends' had tried to have him declared insane. If anyone called asking for him, she was to say that he had been away a month. On Sunday 10 December, when Sergeant Alexander had stood on the doorstep of 94 Great Titchfield Street with Mrs Lincoln telling him that Blatch hadn't been there in a month, the man he wanted to question had been standing at the upper window looking down on him. Blatch was not a wanted man at the time, neither did Alexander have any right of entry to

Essex police superintendent, c. 1910. (Essex Police Museum)

the property, but it was still a painfully humiliating realisation. Blatch had departed that afternoon – where, no one knew – and on the following day Elizabeth Rash left by cab.

The new information was distributed to the cab firms, and this time bore fruit. On 27 December, Inspector Summons, Sergeant Alexander and a Scotland Yard detective went to 80 Harrow Road. There, in an upstairs room they found Elizabeth Sarah Rash. She was staying with a female friend, and of Arthur Blatch there was no sign. Among the items found in the house were the wicker basket, a camera, a full length man's coat, a black and white check cap, a canvas case containing a camera tripod, and some Trichinopoly cigars. The camera, its case and the tripod were those used by Blatch. The cap was later identified as the property of Josiah Nunn, Welch's porter, who had left it in the shop on the night of the fire. The cigars were of a kind smoked by Welch and kept by him in his office. The coat undoubtedly belonged to Blatch, and bloodstains were found on the sleeve.

Mrs Lincoln had been found out in a serious lie, and like so many liars tried to excuse herself by telling more lies. She first of all stated that she had not lied at all, as she had only said that Blatch didn't live there, not that she hadn't seen him, and denied knowing that he was in the house when Alexander had called. Although identified by Alexander as the person he had spoken to she tried to claim that she was ill in bed when he arrived and it was her daughter who had seen him. Charged with the fact that she had known from 15 December that Blatch was wanted for murder, and had still stuck to her story, she was eventually reduced to citing influenza, old age, bad memory and simple mistake. She made a pathetic showing at the resumed inquest.

By contrast, Elizabeth Rash gave her evidence clearly and honestly. When Blatch had returned from Colchester on 9 December she had asked him if he had bought his new clothes from Welch's and he had at once turned very pale. She noted that the shirt he was wearing had had the wrist bands torn off but when she asked to have it for a cleaning cloth he removed it and put it on the fire. After dinner he had taken some packages from his pocket wrapped up in newspaper. The contents consisted of some £80 in gold coin (worth well over £5,000 today) which he counted out on the table, then returned to his pockets, refusing to say how he had come by it. The basket she said had previously been kept in Colchester at his wife's house, and he had told her that when there he had been to Chapel Street and collected it, a visit which Mrs Blatch had failed to mention to the police.

Mrs Lincoln, said Elizabeth, had spoken to Blatch about Sergeant Alexander's visit. Immediately afterwards Blatch had put the two purses of money in his pockets, then, saying he was going into the country for a few days, he departed in the direction of Euston station. She never saw him again. Afterwards she found that he had left her a sovereign and six half sovereigns. On the Monday Mrs Lincoln had accosted her, mentioning the lie she had told on Blatch's behalf and warned her to stick to the story.

With the evidence all in, the inquest jury on 11 January 1894 had no hesitation about bringing in a unanimous verdict of 'wilful murder' against Arthur Blatch, with a recommendation that Mrs Lincoln should not be allowed her expenses and that she should be handed over to the police for

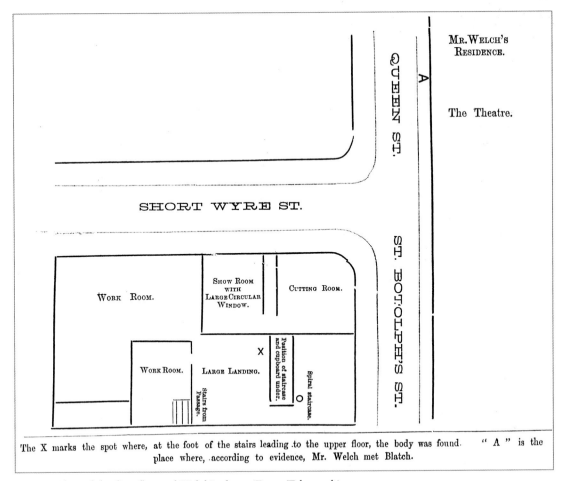

The X marks the spot where, at the foot of the stairs leading to the upper floor, the body was found. "A" is the place where, according to evidence, Mr. Welch met Blatch.

Plan of the first floor of Welch's shop. (Essex Telegraph)

suitable action, a comment that provoked considerable applause. Mr White, the Welch family solicitor, gave particular thanks to Drs Laver and Cook at whose instance Dr Bond had been summoned, as he felt that without their contribution his friend might have gone to his grave with the stigma of suicide on his head. (This comment gave rise to some grittily polite but pointed correspondence in the newspapers, in which Becker and Maybury claimed they had suspected foul play from the start, but that their opinion had been ignored by the police; Coombs denied ignoring them, and still others suggested that it was Laver's and Cook's insistence on bringing in Bond that had created the delay that enabled Blatch to escape.) It only remained to commit Arthur Blatch for trial on the charge of murder at the next assizes following his eventual arrest.

Soon afterwards Mrs Blatch admitted that her husband had been hiding in her house for four days prior to the murder and had actually been there on the day of the crime. Despite the fact that it was a four room house, of which two were occupied by lodgers, it was rumoured that he might still be there, and the house was besieged by large numbers of local people, peering through the windows all hoping for the £50 reward for the wanted man's capture.

A new portrait and description of Blatch was issued and widely circulated. Reports flooded in from all over the country that Blatch had been spotted or even actually arrested. Men of a similar appearance admitted to workhouses, seen behaving eccentrically, or found dead were reported to be Blatch until a cursory examination showed otherwise.

The murder weapon, which would be a vital piece of evidence in the event of a trial, had still not been conclusively identified. The suspected item was a crowbar, which did not belong to the shop, but was something Blatch might have used in his work as a porter. It was coated with rust, and it was then thought impossible to detect the presence of blood on an item where much rust was present. It was Dr Becker who devised a new test which confirmed the presence of blood on the crowbar, and his work was published in the *British Medical Journal*.

Every so often there was a rumour of Blatch's arrest. He was said to have been seen in America and Australia, and in 1898 he was confidently stated to be in Greece, but this, like all the other reports, came to nothing. As the century drew to its close, it seemed that Blatch had got away free, and then reports began to trickle in that he might be in New Zealand. Their origin was the statement of a Colchester woman named Margaret Archer, a farmer's daughter born in 1866, who, so far from claiming reward or fame, was terrified of the implications of her story. She had once been an employee of Welch's shop, and had had some romantic involvement with Blatch. Some five years previously when visiting Wellington, she had recognised her old flame. She had spoken to him, and he had confessed to the murder of Welch. She had not informed against him out of fear and the story had only come to light when she had confided in another person who had gone to the police. The police undertook to keep her identity secret and she went into hiding somewhere in deepest Surrey.

The police informant was a Mr Drawbridge, a commercial traveller formerly of Colchester and a friend of Mr Welch. He had sent a statement to Scotland Yard, and detectives had interviewed Miss Archer on her return home. She declared that the man in question had been working as a painter and decorator under the name of Charles Lillywhite, but he was actually Arthur Blatch. In November 1901 Lillywhite was arrested. Drawbridge was present at the occasion and positively identified Lillywhite as Blatch. Lillywhite claimed that while born in England, he was a naturalised American citizen, and that at the time of Welch's murder he had been living in Tacoma, Washington. He had left England in 1885 and had not been back since. He denied knowing Margaret Archer.

There was huge excitement in Colchester, but Head Constable Coombs was cautious. He determined that two men who knew Blatch by sight should be sent to New Zealand to question the prisoner, at an outlay of some £300 to £400. They were Police Sergeant Robert Frost, who had frequently seen Blatch when employed at the recreation ground, and John Marsh, Keeper of the Town Hall, Colchester who had also known Blatch when he had been employed by the Corporation. Meanwhile another witness had appeared, in the shape of 31-year-old Horace Attwood. His late father was a Colchester wine merchant who had once employed Blatch as a potman before he had been the caretaker of the recreation ground. The passage of time naturally made identification difficult, but after Attwood had held a prolonged conversation with the prisoner he declared that he was inclined to believe that the man was Blatch. Yet another witness said she had seen the prisoner with a woman whose luggage was labelled 'Margaret Archer'. It took just seven hours for the news that Lillywhite had been identified as Blatch to cross the globe by cable from Wellington to Colchester.

At the end of February 1901 Frost and Marsh finally arrived in New Zealand, and both soon appeared in court to give their formal identification of the prisoner. It had been eight or nine years since they had seen Blatch and naturally both were somewhat cautious, aware that his appearance might have changed over time. Frost, although unable to be completely positive, felt that the more he saw the prisoner the more he was convinced that he was Blatch. Marsh was more certain, and had concluded that the accused man was indeed Blatch. The difficulty was that Lillywhite was bearded which Blatch never had been. The accused was accordingly taken away and shaved, and seeing him beardless, Frost and Marsh were even more certain that he was Blatch. It was their evidence together with that of Drawbridge that decided matters, and the prisoner was surrendered to take his trial in England. While Frost and Marsh tried to find a shipping line prepared to

WHERE THE BODY WAS FOUND.

This sketch is from a Photo by Mr. G. A. OLDHAM, of Colchester, and represents the interior of the premises after the fire. The spot marked X shows where the body was found. The room was a sort of lumber room, the door of which is seen on the right.

The burned interior of Welch's shop. (Colchester Gazette)

transport them and their prisoner, the newspapers were in a ferment of expectation and speculation, but there were a few voices of quiet sanity. Mrs Louisa Lillywhite, sister-in-law of the Charles Lillywhite who had left England in 1885, and Percy, his nephew, wrote to the press to state that the real Charles Lillywhite had left a number of personal items with his family for safekeeping. The man in custody should therefore be asked to identify what these were.

The party did not arrive in England until 16 June. Two days later Charles Lillywhite was formally charged under the name Arthur Blatch with the murder of Alfred Welch, but as the proceedings closed, those who had observed him in court commented that both his appearance and demeanour were unlike the wanted man. The triumph had become an uncomfortable charade, and matters were settled shortly afterwards. Isaac Lillywhite had arrived in Colchester and declared the prisoner to be his brother Charles.

On 25 June he was joined by the two sisters and nephew of Charles Lillywhite who viewed the prisoner and at once identified him as their relative. After months of investigation and hundreds of pounds of expenditure the authorities were finally obliged to admit that they had arrested the wrong man. Charles Lillywhite was exactly who he claimed to be. No doubt Mr Drawbridge had been taken in by a superficial resemblance and the affecting tale of Margaret Archer. She had claimed that Lillywhite was exactly like the Blatch she had known except for one small detail – he had chemically changed the colour of his eyes. It was an aspect of her story which while initially regarded as suspicious, had somehow got lost in the excitement. Frost and Marsh, having come half way round the world at public expense and with so much resting on their words, had been unable to admit in public that it was all a horrible mistake and had managed to convince themselves that they had their man.

Charles Lillywhite, basking in his new freedom and reunited with his family, was happy to let the question of compensation be settled out of court between the governments of Great Britain and his adopted United States.

Arthur Blatch was never found.

7

TRAGEDY AT SOUTHEND, 1922

The Essex coast, where not bordered by the flat bleakness of salt marshes, has some pleasant sandy beaches ideal for the holiday-maker, and one of its most popular resorts is Southend-on-Sea. The location, on the northern bank of the Thames estuary, has been populated since ancient times. In the early eighteenth century it was still little more than a fishing village, but from 1768 efforts were made to attract visitors for sea-bathing. In the 1790s a hotel and a terrace were constructed, and the town soon met with royal approval. Princess Charlotte, the young daughter of the Prince of Wales, the future King George IV, was there in 1801 on the advice of her doctors, and her mother Queen Caroline found time in her scandal-strewn life to pay a visit in 1803. The year 1829 saw the laying of the first stone of the original Southend Pier, but the real impetus to the town's rapid expansion was the introduction of the railways, bringing Southend and its attractions within easy reach of the East End of London. City dwellers longing to escape grime, pollution and the humdrum working day and seeking fresh air, sea breezes and the open space of the rolling ocean, soon found that Southend had everything they needed just a short train-ride away.

The seaside means pleasure and relaxation, yet there is another more sinister side. The interface between the land and the sea is the border between two worlds, one familiar and hospitable, the other cold and unknown. In just one step, a line may be crossed into something alien, exciting and possibly dangerous. Maybe that is why people sometimes go to the coast not just to bathe and take the bracing air, but to act out some of the great tragedies of their lives.

February would seem an unlikely month for a trip to the English seaside, whatever its purpose, but the February of 1922 was unusually mild, with daytime temperatures reaching the high 50s°F. On 13 February 37-year-old George Pearce and his 24-year-old lady friend, Alice Vincent, having spent a pleasant few days at the Victoria Hotel on the Eastern Esplanade, retired to their rooms where, after asking for a kiss, he suddenly knocked her to the ground and, seizing a razor, commenced a murderous attack. As he sat astride her, aiming wild sweeps at her throat, she screamed, and defended herself gamely, warding off the worst of it, but she would undoubtedly have been overcome and killed if help had not been near. The hotel proprietor burst into the room, and thrusting Pearce aside, rescued the shocked young woman, her face deeply slashed, and minus an earlobe. By the time the police arrived,

Sea front and Marine Parade, Southend-on-Sea, early twentieth century. (Author's Collection)

Pearce, who was depressed after losing his job, had swallowed a fatal dose of carbolic. Twelve days after the regrettable end to George and Alice's holiday, another affectionate couple booked into a boarding house at 14 Grover Street, Southend as Mr and Mrs Palmer.

John Thomas Hilton Palmer was thirty-eight years old, and had for many years worked as a salesman for Kodak. He was based at their head office, on Kingsway, London, where he had achieved a position of some responsibility. On 26 December 1911 he had married Emily Reeves, who was six years his junior, and the couple settled at 76 Clarendon Road, Walthamstow. Three children were born, but the marriage was not a happy one. In 1919, for reasons which Mrs Palmer was afterwards most reluctant to describe, the couple separated, but remained on good terms. A formal separation order was obtained before the Stratford Justices, who also directed Palmer to make a contribution of £2 per week (about £75 today) toward the maintenance of his children. Palmer was very fond of his children, and Emily, who was now living at Wellesley Road, Walthamstow, brought them to see him regularly.

Whatever the difficulties with his relationships, on a purely social level Palmer was a popular man, jovial and pleasant company, well-educated, with lively and interesting conversation. The one fault that Emily would admit to was that he was somewhat too fond of drink, but in the light of his later behaviour one can surmise that beneath the bluff exterior was a fragile personality. In October 1921

Palmer's mother died, an event which devastated him. Shortly after the funeral, he went missing. He was discovered in a hospital two weeks later where he had been taken after an accident, and claimed he had no memory of where he had been or what he had done. The following month he suffered another mysterious accident. He was found unconscious in Moorgate, with a large gash on his head, and had been taken to St Bartholomew's Hospital and X-rayed. He was unable to explain how the accident had happened.

Palmer remained in hospital a fortnight. Ever since that event he had suffered from persistent headaches, and was presumably unable to work, as for a time he could not pay the £2 per week maintenance to his wife. Not that this led to bad feeling. Emily, who remained concerned for his welfare, went to see him in hospital. When he was discharged he went to lodge with his married sister Sarah Fricker and her husband at 35 Blurton Road, Clapton. Emily visited him there, taking the children. Before long, it seemed that for the Palmers, affection had been rekindled, and the comforts of family life beckoned. At the very least Emily must have felt duty-bound to care for her sick husband, and he would have seen that returning to the fold made practical sense. One happy result of the accident was that Palmer appeared to have forsaken alcohol. They started to discuss the possibility of living together again. Palmer's sister and brother-in-law were delighted, as they had been trying to get the couple reunited for some time. By Christmas it was effectively decided that Palmer and his wife would again live together and they started to write letters in an effort to find a suitable place to house the family. Palmer was well enough to go back to work, and the maintenance payments to his wife resumed.

One person who seemed especially pleased at the proposed reunion was 27-year-old Mary Gertrude Baker. Her sweetheart was lodging at the Frickers' and she was therefore a regular visitor there. Mary expressed great fondness for the Palmers' children, and on being told of the plans for the couple to live together, said she was looking forward to this event, and hoped that when they did she would be able to visit them. Mary had no occupation, but lived with her father

Essex police constable, c. 1916. (Essex Police Museum)

88

James Thomas Baker, a packer, at 250 Mile End Road, Stepney, and kept house for him.

Mary had first been introduced to Palmer by her sweetheart just before Christmas 1921, and shortly afterwards had mentioned him to her brother in terms that suggested that all was not as well as it appeared. Although the only problem in Palmer's life at that time appeared to be the persistent headaches resulting from the accident, headaches which his doctors had told him should disappear within the year, Mary described Palmer as a man who appeared to have a considerable worry. Ominously, he had told her that he was afraid that there was going to be a crash in his life. Mary's brother did not meet Palmer until the following February and found him a most likeable man, impressed both by his pleasant manners and interesting conversation. There was no sign of any impending crash, but there were indeed pressures in John Palmer's life of which only one other person knew. Unstable situations can exist in uneasy equilibrium almost indefinitely until events upset the balance. The death of his mother had undoubtedly resulted in a severe depression, and in his efforts to put his life together he had unfortunately run in two mutually exclusive directions. A stronger man might have taken action to resolve matters. A more stable man might at least have allowed events to unfold around him and taken the consequences. John Palmer was neither strong nor stable. At the start of 1922 he was a tragedy waiting to happen, and the only question was, what the tragedy would be, and who would be the sufferer.

In the last week of February John Palmer was absent from work, on the grounds that he was suffering from a bad cold. On Saturday 25th he seemed better, and went out, telling his sister that he was going for a shave and would be back in half an hour. He did not return.

That same Saturday Mary told her brother she was going out to tea with some friends. He later said that although she looked unwell, she was in good spirits. None of her family was aware that her plans were very different, and when she did not return that night, were naturally concerned. Presumably they checked with all the friends she might have visited, and discovered that none of them had seen her or knew where she might be. Having heard nothing from her by the following Monday, they went to the police and reported her missing. After making further enquiries they learned (it is not known how or where) that Mary had been seen in the company of a man, and it was found to everyone's great surprise that the man was John Palmer. It seems that no one, not Mary's brother, or her father, who had also met Palmer, or Palmer's sister, and certainly not Palmer's wife, had any inkling that the two had a relationship other than casual friendship.

Late on Saturday night, Palmer and Mary were brought to Mrs Roper's boarding house in Southend by a railway porter. They gave the landlady the impression that they were a married couple and over the next few days Palmer spoke often and affectionately of his children, and Mary mentioned them in

Marine Parade, Southend-on-Sea, early twentieth century. (Author's Collection)

the same way. They did not appear to be short of funds, and were able to pay 33s in advance for the occupation of a bed-sitting room. Thereafter they paid for their lodgings on a day-by-day basis. They also drank a good deal. On Monday morning when Mrs Roper cleaned the room she found four empty port wine bottles. The couple had originally intended to stay until the Tuesday, but that morning Mary told Mrs Roper she intended to persuade Palmer to stay another night. They went out that day but returned at 1.30 p.m. when Mrs Roper saw that Palmer was fuddled with drink and advised him to lie down while she made him some tea. Mary said he had been drinking port. When they left the lodgings at 1 p.m. on Wednesday Mrs Roper cleaned the room and found another six empty port wine bottles.

What Mrs Roper did not know was that her guests had spent all but their last penny. During their last day together they decided to end it all, to cross the line into another and hopefully better world by stepping into the sea; so at 10 p.m. they went to the beach. There was one snag. The tide was out. People have been known to give up all idea of suicide at such a basic setback, but instead, Mary and Palmer sat themselves down in a shelter on the Marine Parade and waited. Palmer opened their eleventh and last bottle of port wine, which they consumed.

Between 12.30 and 1 a.m. on what was by then the morning of 2 March, PC Reenen was on his regular patrol of the Marine Parade when he saw something on the beach by the water's edge. Flashing his lantern on the object he was horrified to find it was the body of a young woman. A quick examination showed that she was alive, but unconscious, her clothing saturated with sea water. He dragged her to a shelter and attempted to revive her. A few minutes later Sergeant Drage arrived. Mary was beginning to regain consciousness. As her eyes fluttered half open she saw the figure of a man before her and whispered 'is that you, sweetheart?' Although Mary appeared to be recovering it was apparent that there was more the matter with her than a simple soaking. Drage asked her if she had taken anything and she admitted to drinking port wine and Easton's syrup (a popular tonic of the time which contained a small amount of strychnine). At this point it must have seemed to them that they were dealing with nothing more than a drunken slightly drugged woman who had fallen into the sea and it was just a matter of getting her safely home. They asked her where her hat was (in 1922 a hatless woman was, by definition a woman who had lost her hat) and she pointed to the beach. Drage turned his lantern to where she was pointing and saw something else, the body of a man

floating at the edge of the tide. Quickly they dragged the body onto the beach. Drage started artificial respiration and told Reenan to go for help. Checking Mary once more, Reenen noticed an odd smell on her breath. 'You have taken poison,' he said. 'Yes,' she admitted, 'some tabloids [tablets]'. Reenen ran for assistance and soon found a night watchman. When he returned, Drage was still performing artificial respiration on the man. Mary, now very ill, was taken to the watchman's hut where she was given an emetic. As soon as it had acted she was removed to the Victoria Hospital, but there had never been any hope for John Palmer. The exhausted policemen realised that Palmer was dead, and his body was removed to the mortuary. Drage examined the man's clothing and found a cigarette case, a safety razor and some letters which Mary later admitted were in her handwriting. The only money in Palmer's pockets was a penny.

At daylight the Marine Parade was searched and an empty port wine

Essex police sergeant, c. 1925. (Essex Police Museum)

Police lantern, c. 1920. (Essex Police Museum)

bottle was found in one of the shelters together with a gold-plated wedding ring.

On Thursday afternoon Drage went to see Mary in the hospital, cautioned her, and told her that she would probably be charged with attempting to commit suicide, which was then a criminal offence. Mary made a statement which was later read out at the inquest.

We both came to Southend last Saturday, and lodged at 14 Grover Street as man and wife. I am single. I have known Jack about six months. We spent all our money yesterday and decided at 10 o' clock to finish it. After we bought a bottle of port wine we went down and waited for the tide to come in. Both of us had some Easton's syrup, and some tabloids which Jack used for photographs. Then we went into the sea. I was knocked down and came back.

Mary added that the wedding ring had been hers. Palmer had bought it for her but she had removed it before going into the water as she did not want to be found wearing it. The decision to commit suicide had, she said, been mutual. They had decided it was no good going on any further.

The *Southend-on-sea Observer* described the incident as 'A strange tragedy, sordid in some respects, but pathetic in others'. It had caused some excitement in Southend, and many of the locals or visitors turned out to view the scene of the drama. One such was Harold Berridge, a young boy who found two phials on the beach containing tablets used in photography marked 'Poison', and turned them in to the police.

The first that Mary's family knew of her whereabouts was when they received a telegram at 5 a.m. on Thursday morning to say that she was in hospital at Southend, and asking for her relatives to go there at once. The family was very shocked, and it was decided that her father would go to Southend at once. Mrs Palmer and Sarah Fricker went down to Southend to identify the body.

At 10.30 a.m. on 3 March Chief Inspector Crockford went to see Mary in hospital. He had a hard task to perform. Mary was already aware that she had committed a criminal offence in her suicide attempt, but he was now obliged to explain a law she may not have been aware of, that the survivor of a suicide pact is, by a principle known as transfer of malice, considered to be guilty of murder. 'I am going to arrest you on a charge of the wilful murder of John Thomas Hilton Palmer,' he said, giving her the usual caution. Mary could only reply, pathetically, 'I didn't do anything to him'.

When Mary was released from hospital, Crockford took her to the police station, where she was formally charged and cautioned

Harold Berridge, who found the poison on the beach. (Southend Standard)

again. She then made a full statement, rather different in tone and content from the earlier one. No longer was the suicide attempt a mutual decision – gone was the romance – Mary was now saying that the whole thing was Palmer's idea and she had been coerced.

I went out on Saturday to go and see a friend, and he was waiting at the top. He said 'Come out for a little while' and after we had been out he suggested we should come down to Southend. When we got to Liverpool Street he went into a chemist's shop and said he was going to get some Easton's syrup as a tonic for his heart. After taking some himself he gave me some. For almost a fortnight before, he talked of committing suicide and said he could not live as he was in debt and could not leave me behind. He kept on persuading me to take the Easton's syrup, and then he gave me port wine, and I did not know what I was doing. We both got into the water together and then I tried to pull him out but I couldn't. I had a bad throat and could not call out. I didn't have strength

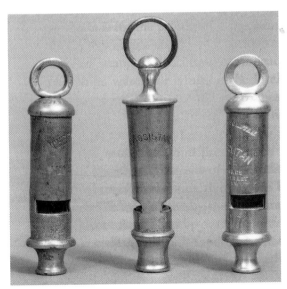

Police whistles, c. 1900. (Essex Police Museum)

The inquest jury on its way to see the body of John Palmer. (Southend Standard)

enough to get up on to the beach. I didn't know any more after I got a little way out of the water. When we went in I did not not know what I was doing, as I had had the port. He would not let me go out alone, and every time I said anything about it he said 'If anyone looks at you I'll smash their face in'.

Half an hour later Mary was in the police court for the preliminary hearing. The magistrates were H.A. Dowsett and W.J. Francis. A slightly built woman, she looked pale and small, and since she felt faint was allowed to be seated. The circumstances of the case were recounted by the chief constable, Mr Kerslake, and Inspector Crockford. Kerslake said that he proposed asking for a week's remand. The case would have to be referred to the Department of Public Prosecutions, and the police would have to await his instructions as to the course they would have to take the following Friday. Asked if she wanted to question the policeman Mary silently shook her head. She was remanded and was led out by a female probation officer.

The inquest was opened on 4 March at the Park Hotel before Mr C. Edgar Lewis, the coroner. Although Mary had been given the opportunity to attend she chose not to. Emily Palmer was there, however, described by the *Southend Standard* as 'a worried-looking woman'. Miss Baker, she said, had treated her husband like an ordinary acquaintance. She had last seen her husband alive on 24 February, the day before he left, and he had seemed in good spirits, apart from complaining about the pains in his head which he attributed to the accident. She had no idea he was carrying on with anybody else. She still had in her pockets the letters she had written as part of the search for a new family home.

Asked the reason for the separation she could only say 'I would rather not mention it – it was nothing to do with anything like this', and denied that it was connected with Palmer's drinking.

Dr F.G. Walker told the court that death was due to asphyxia accelerated by a heart condition. The tongue of the deceased had been blackened which suggested he had taken poison, but it was impossible to say what effect this had had. The two tubes of photographic tablets were produced. One was still full, but some tablets had been removed from the other which contained a silver preparation he did not think to be very deadly.

Drage told the court of his discovery of the body and his interviews with Mary, saying that the woman had had no money on her. The letters found in Palmer's pocket he said 'were all on the loving side'. From their tone he thought that the woman was infatuated. In one letter she had written that she 'was waiting for the time she could have him for always'. The coroner said it was impossible to conclude the inquest that day and it was adjourned for further enquiries to be made, to the discomfiture of the jury who, all being businessmen pleaded that the next hearing be either on a Monday or a Wednesday. The jury was duly reconvened on the following Thursday, when Mary's statement was read to the court.

The coroner, ignoring the implications of Mary's original statement, took the view that the man had prevailed upon the woman to do what she did, and he thought that the jury would think the same. The only proper verdict was one of suicide in regard to the man, but in view of the impending prosecution, they should not refer to the woman. He added that if matters had been the other way around, had the woman died and the man survived he might have directed them another way.

The jury returned a verdict on John Palmer of suicide during temporary insanity, and the coroner commended the actions of PC Reenan and Sergeant Drage.

On Friday Mary was brought before the Justices on charges of wilfully murdering Palmer and attempted suicide. Mrs Palmer sat at the back of the court, dressed in black, and in tears. Mary's father appeared, and was questioned by the chairman. If Mary came back to him would he look after her, and did he think she would settle down? Baker said he thought she would and promised to look after her to the best of his ability. Mary then expressed the desire to go home.

The chairman Mr J.W. Burrows now addressed the prisoner.

PC Reenan, who discovered Mary Baker at the water's edge. (Southend Standard)

Although this is a very serious offence which you have committed, we feel you have had considerable punishment, and we do not desire to prolong the agony. We wish you to realise that excursions of this nature usually end in the position in which you find yourself today. Pull yourself together, settle down, and get into a happy and contented frame of mind.

The murder charge was dropped, and Mary was discharged into the care of her father. For the offence of attempted suicide she was placed on probation.

8

THE BEAST OF HORNCHURCH, 1939

The years from 1925 to 1939 were a period of rapid urbanisation for what had been the predominantly rural village of Hornchurch. Local farmers sold land to developers who were building affordable housing for commuters to London or workers in light industries. Elm Park, dubbed by its creators the 'Wonder town of homes', was built on former agricultural land in the mid-1930s and was then the largest private housing development in Britain. Most houses had five rooms: a sitting room, a kitchen and three bedrooms. The terraced homes cost £395 (about £20,500 now), and the weekly mortgage payment was 11s (or about £125 per month today). A new railway station, Elm Park, was created on the District line to serve the growing estate, and the Elm Park shopping centre was completed by 1939.

In that year Hornchurch Council reported that the town had a population of over 90,800, which was steadily increasing. The official Hornchurch Guide for 1939 must have gone to press before the events of that January, for it stated 'The town has not figured prominently in the stream of national events; being off the beaten track in days gone by, it has perforce pursued the even tenor of its way comparatively unnoticed'. That calm everyday atmosphere of families, factories and leisure was soon to be destroyed, and replaced with terror, suspicion and lost innocence.

Stanley Coventry was an electrician. A widower with one daughter, Pamela, born on 12 February 1929, he had remarried in December 1935, and after living in Rainham and Dagenham for a time, the family moved to Diban Avenue, Elm Park in 1937. In December 1938 they moved south of the District Line to Morecambe Close. Mrs Edith Coventry must have managed the move without her husband, as Stanley had been working in Scunthorpe, Lincolnshire since November.

Pamela Doreen Coventry, a cheerful and popular girl, with wavy brown hair, was a normal child, perhaps a little shy with strangers, who enjoyed her music lessons each Tuesday in Diban Avenue. She attended the Council school in Benhurst Avenue, which was near enough to Morecambe Close for her to come home for her midday meal. The route from her home lay along South End Road, turning left along the curve of Coronation Drive, passing over the railway bridge of Elm Park station, and through Elm Park shopping centre. From there it was a minute's walk to Diban Avenue and only a little further to the school. At no point in that journey was she potentially out of the view of any passer-by.

Pamela Coventry. (The News)

On 3 January Pamela returned home from her music lesson at 6.30 p.m., and asked her stepmother if she could go on an errand for a man who lived in Coronation Drive. Mrs Coventry showed a quite natural caution, and asked Pamela if she knew the man. Pamela said that she did.

'Where did you meet him?' was the obvious next question.

'As I was coming home from music,' said Pamela, innocently.

This was not Mrs Coventry's definition of 'knowing' the man, and she therefore refused to let Pamela go on the errand. Nothing more was said about the incident.

On Wednesday 18 January Pamela attended morning school as usual, coming home for lunch, which she ate at 12.45. Half an hour later she was on her way back to school.

Although the weather was fairly mild for the time of year, there was a blustery wind, and the constant threat of rain. Mrs Coventry had made sure her step-daughter would not be cold, providing her with warm underclothes and woollen stockings, a thick woollen sweater, and a gymslip which bore the plain yellow badge of her netball team. Pamela's saxe-blue lined swagger coat was fastened with bright white metal ball buttons, and the ensemble was completed by a beret and Wellington boots. Under her arm she carried a brown paper bag containing her dancing shoes. The outside of the bag was printed with the name of 'Leonards', a local boot and shoe repairer. The last time Mrs Coventry saw her stepdaughter alive was as she waved to the little girl, who had just turned into Coronation Drive. Pamela had agreed to meet up with two of her school friends on the far side of the railway at 1.30 p.m., but she didn't show up. Somewhere between the corner of Coronation Drive and the railway bridge, a distance of just over 100yd, Pamela Coventry had disappeared.

The little girls could not have suspected at that point that anything was wrong, and Pamela was marked absent from school. As the children poured out of their classes at the end of the school day, Mrs Coventry went to meet Pamela as had been arranged. It was only then that she discovered that Pamela had not been in school that afternoon. Frantically, she made enquiries among Pamela's friends and teachers, but with no news forthcoming, she reported the child's disappearance to Elm Park police station, and the police at once commenced enquiries.

Mrs Coventry could only return home to wait. A long evening passed, and there was no sign, no news of Pamela. At 10.30 p.m. the rain started to hammer down, and still Pamela did not return. By the following morning Pamela's description had been circulated and widespread searches of the area were being carried out.

When Pamela was found, however, it was by pure chance. At 10.30 a.m. 19 January, Charles Horsman, a night watchman, was cycling down Wood Lane, which was not far from both Morecambe Close and Coronation Drive. There was a deep ditch beside the road, and his elevated position on the bicycle enabled him to see a pale object like a parcel at the bottom of the ditch. He went to investigate, and was shocked to see the naked body of a young girl lying on the rotting remains of an old mattress. She was effectively folded into three, her knees bent and raised to her chin, arms by her sides, her face pressed into the side of the ditch away from the road. She had been trussed – there was no other word for it – with what appeared to be electrical cable. It had passed around her back, over her thighs and shins, trapping her arms, the ends crossed, and then tied around her ankles. The only piece of clothing remaining on her body was her petticoat, which was tied around her neck.

Horsman at once ran to the nearby home of the wing commander of the local RAF station, who telephoned the police. A doctor was called to the spot and certified that the child had been dead for several hours. It was also obvious to him that she had been the victim of a brutal sexual assault. An examination of the surrounding area revealed no sign that the crime had occurred near where the body was found. At first, it was thought that she might have been abducted by car. Scotland Yard detectives were brought in, and both the Metropolitan and Essex Police, assisted by the RAF, scoured the neighbourhood for clues, and in particular for any trace of the missing clothes. Pamela was soon identified, and her father was given the terrible news when he returned home that evening.

The post mortem was carried out by one of the greatest pathologists of his age – Sir Bernard Spilsbury. He revealed that Pamela had been struck on the right lower jaw, probably by a fist. She had then fallen onto a hard surface, hitting the left side of her head, where a bruise was visible. These injuries had not been sufficient to cause her death. However, it was perhaps some small consolation to her family that she may have been unconscious during the rape. Death was due to strangulation. Blood was found in her right nostril.

There were a few vital clues the body had to offer. It was clean, with no marks apart from those of the assault, so the crime must have taken place indoors, somewhere with a covering on the floor. It was also clear from the stomach contents that she had died within an hour of her last known meal, and therefore within half an hour of leaving the house. Although the bottom of the ditch and the mattress were both damp from the previous night's rain, the body itself was dry and must have been taken there after the rain had stopped.

The cable that tied the body was a highly significant clue. Described as seven strand black copper insulated flex, it had attached along its length in places some worn-looking lengths of tarred or creosoted string. It looked as though it might have been used at one time to tie up garden plants such as runner beans. There was also a piece of green cable, with similar string attached. When the body was extended one more extraordinary clue was found. Pressed between one thigh and the chest was a cigarette-end. It could only have been dropped there by the killer. It was not a commercially available brand but was hand rolled.

Efforts were made to discover more about the green and black cable. The green variety, it was found, was of a type still being manufactured, but the black cable had not been made in the last twelve years. Both pieces were photographed and the pictures published in the national press, but while many helpful people came forward with suggestions, this line of enquiry did not bear fruit.

Although the full details of Pamela's injuries were not revealed in the press, terrified parents drew their own conclusions, and most were convinced that the killer was a local man. Younger pupils were forbidden to go to and from school unaccompanied, and anxious mothers flocked around schools at the end of lessons to collect their children and escort them safely home. No one was free of suspicion – no one could be trusted until the man was caught. The news revealed some uncomfortable aspects of life on the Elm Park Estate. The police had known for some months that there were men in the area accosting women and children, and pupils attending Suttons School had found letters on paths offering money to children who would meet the writer in some lonely country lane. Yet Pamela was the kind of girl who would not have gone meekly with someone she did not know and trust.

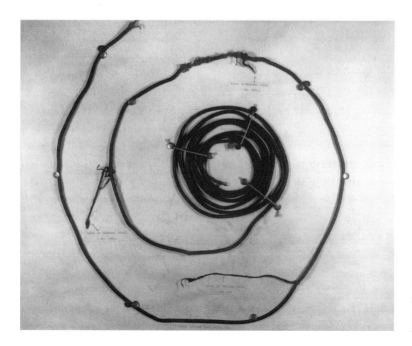

The cable used to tie up Pamela Coventry. (Essex Police Museum)

Elm Park mothers collecting their children from school. (The News)

What had been a local case was now a nationwide enquiry. Some obvious suspects were questioned and released, and a few unstable persons offered manifestly false confessions. The police were coming to the conclusion that it was highly unlikely that any of Pamela's clothes would be discovered, when on 21 January Pamela's Wellingtons were found in a ditch in Abbs Cross Lane, ¾ mile from Morecambe Close. They were in a paper bag printed with the name of 'Leonards'. This find completely revised the theory that the murder had happened elsewhere. The police were now sure that the killer was a local man. They had been searching for clues in the vicinity of Pamela's home and the ditch where the body was discovered, but this deliberate placing of the boots seemed an obvious ploy to try and move the focus of enquiries away from what must be the haunt or indeed the home of the killer.

Pamela's mention of the man in Coronation Drive had not been forgotten, especially as school friends of Pamela reported that a few days before her death they had seen her talking to a man there. As the weather deteriorated, the police, hampered by heavy snowstorms, went out with a questionnaire for householders, and made house-to-house calls all along Coronation Drive to discover the movements of the residents between the crucial hours of 1 p.m. and 2 p.m. on 18 January. They also questioned Walter Gynn, the milkman who delivered there, and he had some interesting statements to make about one of his customers.

Leonard Richardson was twenty-eight years old, a married man with two small children. On 9 January his wife Ivy had been admitted to hospital to give birth to their second child, and she did not return home with their new baby girl until 22 January. The oldest child, a boy aged three and a half, had been cared for by his wife's sister, and another sister, Mrs Lilian Gray, called in during the day to cook his meals and do the housework. Richardson had effectively been left to his own devices for much of the time, and had taken the opportunity to do some decorating. He was a shift-worker at the May and Baker chemical factory in Dagenham, a journey of some fifteen minutes by bicycle, and about the same if he went by train, which he only did in bad weather. The week commencing 9 January Richardson had been on the early shift, working from 6 a.m. to 3 p.m. and it was arranged that Gynn would call him at 5 a.m. when he delivered the milk. The following week, however, Richardson was working the late shift, from 2 p.m. to 11 p.m., and told Gynn not to call him early again. Gynn recalled seeing Richardson at 1.15 p.m. on 18 January, leaving a café and riding his bicycle down South End Road away from Coronation Drive. Richardson, who had been wearing a raincoat, had nodded his head at Gynn as he passed. At the top of Wood Lane, however, he had stopped, and for some reason had turned around and ridden back to Coronation Drive. Gynn had not seen him again that day. The following morning Gynn had been delivering milk as usual, and to his surprise, saw the light burning in the kitchen of Richardson's house. It was then only 5.20 a.m.

Pamela's funeral was held on 26 January at Barking cemetery. Her death had deeply affected the whole community. Residents of Elm Park estate had organised collections to provide floral tributes, and children gave their pennies at school. The amounts collected were so generous that there was an excess, which was put towards the cost of the headstone. An estimated 2,500 people, hoping perhaps to show what emotional support they could, lined the streets at Elm Park to see the cortège of ten cars pass by, and in Barking a crowd of 5,000 had to be marshalled by the police to try and ensure some measure of privacy for the Coventry family. At the graveside, relatives, overcome by a grief beyond comprehension, collapsed weeping and had to be carried away.

On 26 January Richardson was questioned about his movements. Told that he could smoke if he liked, he rolled himself a cigarette. A few minutes later the cigarette, tobacco pouch and papers were removed from him. Fourteen stubs were found in his tobacco pouch and one in the pocket of his jerkin. He had been in the habit of saving the stubs and using them to roll new cigarettes. All the tobacco evidence was later handed over to Mr Jollyman, an expert at the chemical laboratory at the Imperial Tobacco Co., Bristol. Richardson cooperated fully in giving a statement. As he did so Inspector Bridger noticed that he had an abrasion on the knuckle of the small finger of both hands. The one on the right hand was old and healing, but the one on the left was recent.

Richardson had lived in Coronation Drive for two or three years, and was familiar with the Elm Park area. Until nine months ago, he said, he had used a route to work which took him through Wood Lane. Learning that a better way was to cycle south past Wood Lane and turn off at Ford Lane, he had used that route ever since. To arrive at work for a 2 p.m. start he would normally have set out at about 1.25 p.m. On Monday 16th he had suffered an accident at work. A still had bubbled over and his eyes and throat had been affected by the fumes. This had not, however, been serious enough to prevent him working or cycling home in the usual way. He had arrived home at 11.20 p.m. and had been up painting the kitchen until 3 a.m.

He could not recall how he had gone to work on Tuesday, but he was certain he had gone by train on Wednesday. His home was only a few minutes walk from Elm Park station, and the journey was just three minutes to Dagenham where his place of work was right next to the station.

That day he had got up at 9.30 a.m. and after breakfast continued the decorating. While busy with this, his sister-in-law had come and cooked a meal for him, departing between 1 p.m. and 1.30 p.m. He was feeling unwell, and thought he might have caught a cold, nevertheless he decided to go to work, and left at 1.40 p.m., not by bicycle, but to get the train at Elm Park station. He had arrived at work just before 2 p.m., and found that the man working the early shift had also been affected by the fumes and had gone home.

Richardson contacted the works manager and told him he had suffered a similar accident and was feeling unwell. He was given permission to go home, which he did, arriving at 3 p.m. Mrs Gray called shortly afterwards to collect

The railway bridge, looking towards Elm Park Shopping Centre. (Author's Collection)

her umbrella and do the washing up. He went to bed and remained there until after 5 p.m. then cycled to Elm Park Broadway to try and get some putty. Later that afternoon he went to his doctor in Abbs Cross Lane, saying his eyes were still hurting, and was given a prescription for conjunctivitis. He continued his decorating and was in bed by midnight.

Asked if he had approached a child to run an errand for him, he said that during the first week of his wife being in hospital he had asked a little girl to get some tobacco for him, but the child had run away, and a neighbour had offered to send her daughter instead. Leaving aside the question of whether tobacconists would have sold their wares to small children, this incident as described by Richardson would have happened the week after the event described by Pamela as taking place on 3 January.

Notably omitted from Richardson's statement was any mention of seeing the milkman at 1.15 p.m. on Wednesday, and any explanation of why his light was on so early the following morning.

The story told by Richardson was checked, and corroborated. His neighbour had seen him approach the little girl who had run away, the factory at Dagenham confirmed he had reported the accident on Monday 16 January and clocked in at 1.55 p.m. two days later. His doctor said he had examined Richardson on the Wednesday, and while he had found no trace of any chemical accident he had accepted the story as he thought his patient was suffering from shock and nervousness. The police noted that Dr Steen's surgery was only 100yd from the spot where Pamela's Wellingtons had been found.

One of Richardson's neighbours stated that she had been looking out of her front window some time before 2 p.m. on 18 January and had seen him leave his front gate and start to run towards the railway station. She noticed that he was wearing his cycle clips, and after a while he had stopped to remove them. She recalled the incident because she remembered wondering if his new baby had been taken ill and he was hurrying to the hospital.

On 28 January another discovery was made, when a newspaper-wrapped parcel was seen by a schoolboy crossing over Elm Park railway bridge. It contained a length of rolled-up black cable, identical to that used to tie up Pamela, two metal buttons, and a yellow badge. He was sensible enough to take his find to the police station and a search of the area turned up another button. Mrs Coventry identified the buttons and badge as having come from Pamela's coat and gymslip. The newspaper was an edition of the *News Chronicle* dated 11 January and the parcel was held together by insulation tape. This discovery must have told the police that they would never find Pamela's clothing. The murderer must have disposed of them by burning, removing items such as metal buttons which were non-flammable, and disposing of the rubber Wellingtons which would create noticeable fumes if burnt.

The police felt they had enough evidence to obtain a search warrant for Richardson's home. Every technique then available was used, but the result

Open land at the back of Coronation Drive. (Author's Collection)

was meagre and inconclusive – some tarred string similar to that on Pamela's body, and a run of copies of the *News Chronicle* with the 11 January issue missing. They found nothing to connect Richardson directly with Pamela or the crime scene.

Backing onto Richardson's garden were some half-built houses and a field. From the house to the ditch in Wood Lane where the body had been found was a matter of only 450 paces. The way there was clear and sheltered from the road by a hedge. If Richardson was the killer then the disposal of the body would have been simple.

A few days later the police had a visit from a neighbour of Leonard Richardson who had something he wished to hand in. It was a length of green cable to which was attached a piece of creosoted string. The neighbour, Mr Curley, said Richardson had given it to him the previous December. He had seen Richardson on the evening of 18 January when he had looked unwell, and seemed to have something on his mind. He had mentioned having 'private worries' but did not elaborate. Richardson, said Curley, had also mentioned at Christmas time, that the chemicals in the place he worked aroused sexual feelings. With a heavily pregnant wife, it would not have been too surprising had Richardson been feeling frustrated at that time.

On 1 February Richardson was at work in Dagenham when the police called and arrested him. He was charged with the murder of Pamela Coventry. A detailed examination was made of his clothing, his bicycle and his garden shed. This turned up some green cable with creosoted string attached, and some adhesive tape similar to that which had been around the newspaper. All the evidence was handed to the senior Home Office analyst, Dr Roche Lynch.

Until Richardson's arrest, the newspapers had been declaring that the murder was obviously the work of a maniac, and nothing had occurred to disturb the public image of some lone degenerate targeting children. It came as something of a shock to find that the man in the dock was an apparently normal, happily married man with two children, and from the start, many found it impossible to believe in his guilt.

Richardson made a number of short court appearances over the next few weeks, wearing a grey suit, fawn pullover and striped collar and tie. It must have been his best outfit, for the newspapers commented that he wore the same clothes for every appearance. He seemed always to be composed. His wife and other members of his family always turned up to show their support, and he would wave to them as he left the court. It was at the fourth remand hearing on 24 February, lasting 4½ hours that the prosecution case was laid before the public. This time the newspapers did not decline to describe Pamela's injuries. 'There had,' said Mr Parham, prosecuting, 'been sexual interference with both organs.' The three main items on which the prosecution was relying were the cigarette stub, the cable, and the newspaper-wrapped buttons and badge.

Mrs Gray gave evidence that she had seen Richardson on 18 January when she had cooked his dinner, but had left at about 1.15 p.m. She had later returned, having forgotten her umbrella, and arrived at 2.45 p.m. when he was at home, upstairs. After doing the washing-up she left but went back almost at once, having forgotten her umbrella a second time. She saw nothing unusual on these visits. Since she did not carry a watch, she admitted that she could not swear to the exactness of any of the times. A strong witness for the defence was Mrs Thomason the Richardsons' next door neighbour. She said the dividing walls of the semi-detached houses were thin, and she had heard nothing from the house next door between 1 p.m. and 2 p.m. on the 18th.

At the second hearing on 10 March, Dr Steen stated that he had examined Richardson on the 18th, and found mild conjunctivitis. His patient was of a nervous temperament and had seemed somewhat upset, with a raised pulse rate. Dr Roche Lynch thought the wire handed in by Mr Curley was similar to that found on Pamela's body. There were also similarities between the insulating tape on the parcel and that in the shed, but they were of common makes. He had found about a dozen small spots of human blood on the inside of the right sleeve of Richardson's mackintosh, ranging in size from a pinhead to ⅛in in diameter, and some smears in the lining of his right-hand trouser pocket. He thought there was probably enough blood on the mackintosh to determine the group, but insufficient on the trousers.

Mr Jollyman said he had compared the stub ends found in Richardson's possession to that found on the body. The tobacco, the watermark found on the paper and the method of rolling were all the same. The method of rolling he thought to be unusual – there was a reverse fold at one corner of the paper which made the cigarette smaller at one end than at the other.

Leonard Richardson was committed to stand trial at the Old Bailey. The hearing commenced on 27 March, and the weight of the evidence against him was now exposed to the full glare of the Court. The prosecution submitted that Richardson had had ample time to commit the murder between 1.15 p.m. and 1.45 p.m. and he could then have disposed of the body on the night of the 18th or early the following morning. Gynn gave the same story he had told before. Robustly cross-examined, he would not accept that he could have been mistaken as to the dates.

Mrs Gray gave evidence as before but mentioned that when at Richardson's house, she had used a copy of the *News Chronicle* to light a fire.

Sir Bernard Spilsbury was as firm as ever in court. The defence suggested that the blood spots in the mackintosh could have been caused by the wearer having skinned his knuckles previously. Spilsbury was adamant that the marks he had examined had not been made in that way, as they were distinct spots and not smears. He thought they could have been made when Pamela had breathed her last through a bloody nostril while being strangled.

Roche Lynch, who had been unable to determine blood group on the exhibits, said at the time he had examined them he had been aware of the injury to the defendant's hand. 'I formed the opinion,' he said, 'that they definitely could not be explained by the injury to the finger.'

'Why is the witness asked this question?' demanded the judge. 'This is surely a question for the jury'.

Mr Jollyman also fell foul of Mr Justice Hawke. He had suggested that the tobacco in the stub found on the child's body had been mixed with stub ends but Hawke pointed out that this too was a matter for the jury to decide. 'What you mean is that the tobacco had been charred by heat,' he said, and Jollyman agreed. On being questioned, Jollyman was forced to admit that half the handmade cigarette paper in the country was of the same make as produced in court. Mr Winn for the defence then produced an envelope which he said contained stubs collected from the floor of a workman's messroom. There were eighteen, and of these eleven bore the same characteristic as the one found on the body. He proposed that there was no case to answer, but Mr Justice Hawke stated that only the jury could stop the case if they wished, and so Leonard Richardson entered the witness box.

Richardson gave his evidence well. He said that Gynn must have been mistaken as to the day he had seen him on his bicycle. He had started to cycle to work on the 17th, but after waiting for a friend at the top of Coronation Drive had turned back because it was wet and taken the train instead. If there

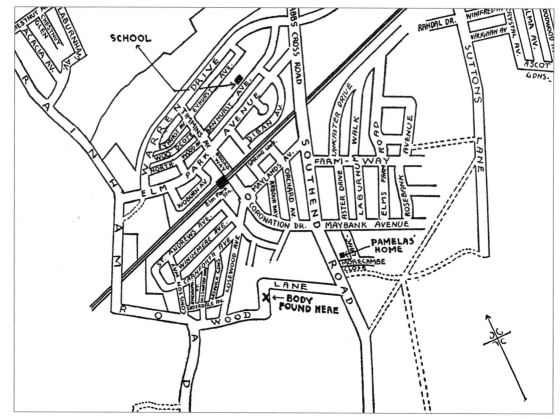

Central Hornchurch, 1939. (The News)

had been a light in his house at 5.20 a.m. on the 19th it must have been left on by accident. He had injured his hands tightening nuts at work. The only thing he couldn't explain was why he had travelled by train on the Wednesday when it wasn't wet. 'I suppose it was one of the times when I broke the rule,' was all he could say. At Winn's request Richardson was given some materials with which to roll a cigarette. Mr Justice Hawke examined it and then handed it to Winn saying that there was a slight 'rucking-back' in it.

Richardson's family now gave evidence. They had bravely and loyally stood by him during his ordeal. Not only had they been convinced of his utter innocence, they had taken their own steps to question some of the prosecution evidence. It was Ivy Richardson who had had the idea of collecting cigarette stubs to show that her husband's method of rolling a cigarette was not unusual. In the fortnight leading up to the trial, she and Richardson's brother had been busy collecting the stubs of hand-rolled cigarettes, some from neighbours, and others from factory floors. They had passed the samples to their solicitor who had asked Frank Hall, general manager of the Rizla Cigarette Paper Co. to examine them. In evidence, he said he had found that many had been rolled with an under turn. The supposedly unusual method of rolling was not as rare as suggested by the prosecution.

A new witness, Mrs Violet Cavalier, a neighbour, also corroborated Richardson's account of his movements on the Tuesday by saying she had shared a train with him that day and he had told her of starting out on his bicycle and then turning back because of the weather.

By lunchtime the jury obviously felt that they had heard enough. Without troubling to hear the closing statements or the judge's summing up they had concluded that there was insufficient evidence on which to find Richardson guilty. When the court re-assembled a note was passed to Mr Justice Hawke as soon as he took his seat. A formal verdict of 'not guilty' was returned, and Leonard Richardson left the court a free man. Outside the courtroom the members of the jury shook hands with him and wished him luck.

Soon afterwards, Leonard Richardson was home enjoying a cup of tea and a cigarette with his family, and praising his wife's detective work. He revealed that while in prison he had received numerous letters of support from workmates and neighbours, many of whom had come to see him, and urged him not to even think of leaving the district after what they were sure was a certain acquittal. His employers had paid his wages during the time he had been in prison, and had kept his job open for him.

As for the future, he told reporters, 'I shall resume my work at Dagenham when I have rested. I shall continue to cycle there. I am buying this house and I shall go on living here.'

The murder of Pamela Coventry remains unsolved, but the Beast of Hornchurch never struck again.

9

EXPLOSION AT RAYLEIGH, 1943

The rolling fields of Essex are ideal grain-growing country, and part of the county's rich heritage are its windmills, many of which have been expertly restored and preserved and are now listed buildings. The tallest windmill in Essex is the Tower Mill at Rayleigh, built in 1809, and was a working windmill well into the twentieth century. In 1906 the sails were taken down, but the mill continued to grind by other means. Local trade directories show that in 1937 Rayleigh Mill was operated by T.J. Brown and Son, and was oil powered.

Archibald Brown, the older son of Thomas James, was born in Rayleigh in 1896. He served three years in the First World War, but at the age of twenty-four had suffered a serious accident while riding a motor cycle. After a long recuperation he appeared to have made a recovery, but the accident had left a weakness in his spine which would return to torment him. In the summer of 1922 Archibald, now employed in his father's business, married 21-year-old Dorothy Lucy Willans, and in October the following year their first son, Eric James, was born. Another son, Colin George, was born in 1927. When Thomas died two years later, leaving £20,405 (about £837,000 today) Archibald took control of the family business.

Rayleigh was changing. Shortly after the end of the war, housing developments began to spring up, bringing in city workers wanting to take advantage of the fast rail service to London, while enjoying the still predominantly rural setting and proximity to coastal resorts. This desirable location was to be something of a drawback when, after the outbreak of the Second World War, south-east Essex became a target for German air raids. Even after the tide of the war had turned in favour of the Allies, enemy action was a constant threat. In April 1943 the *Southend-on-Sea and County Pictorial* reported a raid on the Thames Estuary in which five people died, and on 17 May a bomb landed in the back garden of an Essex bungalow. The occupants, a woman and her three sons, cowering in their Anderson shelter, escaped with minor injuries. Two days later a lone aircraft dropped a bomb in a country district. War news dominated the press, with stirring stories of gallant deeds by Essex men, details of those killed on active service, and exhortations to those at home to conserve vital supplies and invest in war savings.

By then, Archibald Brown had become an invalid, and a grumpy one at that. In the previous five years increasing paralysis of the spine had gradually reduced his mobility to the point where he spent much of his time in bed, and was unable to walk without assistance. His demands were a strain on Dorothy, whose devotion never wavered, and she hired a private nurse to help care for him. Nurse Picken had attended him, then a Nurse Hines, but somehow neither of these suited, and they left. The new nurse was 46-year-old Elsie Irene Mitchell of 12 Hillview Road, Rayleigh. Brown liked her, and she stayed.

The substantial family home, Summerfields, was at 19 London Hill, Rayleigh. Eric had been working at a bank in Rochford, but in June 1942 he left, volunteering for the Royal Navy. While waiting to be called up, he worked on his uncle's farm at Canewdon. When the call came, however, it was from the Army, and he joined up on 1 October 1942, entering the Eighth Battalion of the Suffolk Regiment. He was stationed at Spilsby in Lincolnshire. On 17 May he had returned home for fourteen days leave, but soon after rejoining his unit his mother wrote to his commander asking if he could be granted extended compassionate leave on the grounds of his father's illness, as his condition had worsened. Eric was granted three months leave to enable him to arrange for someone to take over control of his father's business. He returned on 12 July, and spent his days working as a junior hand at the mill.

Normally, Nurse Mitchell attended for night duties only, but in fine weather, she would take her patient for a daytime ride in an invalid chair, ostensibly to enjoy the fresh air, although once outside he liked to light up a cigarette. The chair was kept in the family's air-raid shelter, which had two doors, the inner one of which was never locked. The chair was usually folded away for storage and the bottom was made of canvas stretched over a metal frame, on which rested a seat of brown velveteen.

Archibald Brown took his last ride after lunch on Friday 23 July 1943. The chair was wheeled up to the house, and the invalid, in pyjamas, dressing gown and cap, was led up to it by the two women, who helped him to sit. Two pillows were placed at his back, and a plaid travelling rug and a woollen blanket were laid across his knees, the ends securely tucked under the chair cushion. Nurse Mitchell then wheeled her charge away from the house, down London Hill, and up the Hockley Road. They had proceeded in this pleasant way for about a mile, passing by Rayleigh church, and she had just wheeled him past the junction with Nelson Road, when Brown decided he wanted a cigarette, and made an effort to remove the packet from his dressing gown pocket, shifting his weight in the chair. Nurse Mitchell stopped, walked around in front of him and helped him to light his cigarette. He was settling himself when she returned to the back of the chair.

There was a sudden violent explosion. Her first sensation was of tremendous heat coming up from below, and she smelt her hair burning. The chair, and indeed her patient, seemed to have disappeared. Dazedly she realised that her legs were pumping blood. Then she heard a sound that she was unlikely ever to forget. It was a thump on the road behind her. She turned around. Lying in

Hockley Road, 1943. (Essex Police Museum)

the roadway was the upper half of Archibald Brown. He seemed to have been severed at the waist. She started to scream.

Nearby, the windows at Hedgecroft, the home of a Mr and Mrs Todd, had been blown out by the explosion. Mrs Todd and her maid heard the screams and ran outside. A Mr Fuller, of Little Swakeleys was also quickly on the scene. Nurse Mitchell was taken indoors and given first aid. There were numerous small pieces of metal embedded in her legs. An ambulance was summoned, and the nurse was taken to the Southend Municipal Hospital, Rochford. Miraculously, her injuries were not life threatening, a fact that was attributed to the body of her patient with his surrounding pillows and blankets absorbing a substantial amount of the shock.

Police and bomb wardens soon arrived and surveyed the carnage on Hockley Road. That there had been a sizeable explosion there could be no doubt. The lower torso of Archibald Brown had been shattered into bloody fragments, and both legs were torn off at the hip joint. One had been thrown 48ft and landed in a front garden, the other had travelled 30ft and come to rest in the branches of a tree some 15ft off the ground. The blast had left several holes in the road. The chair was a mangled wreck, the wheels and frame twisted, the back torn, but of the canvas seat and its velveteen cushion there was no sign – they, like those parts of Archibald which had rested on them, had been blown to pieces. A magnetic examination of the pitted roadway turned up some metal fragments which had clearly not belonged to the chair, and the largest of these were handed over to a military explosives expert for examination.

It was understandable that the first reaction to the incident was that the explosion was due to enemy action. The *Southend-on-Sea and County Pictorial* reported in its stop press column that Brown had been killed when a low-flying plane dropped a bomb. Other newspapers, which must have checked first and found that no aircraft had been reported in the area, stated that the wheel of the chair had struck something hidden in the grass verge which had exploded. The examination of the human remains and of the chair told a different and disturbing story.

The post mortem, which was carried out by Dr Gilmour at Southend Municipal Hospital on the following day, concluded un-surprisingly that death was due to multiple injuries caused by an explosion. It was clear, however that the detonation had not happened at ground level, but had been immediately below the victim's buttocks. The explosive device, whatever it was, had been within the very framework of the chair, between the seat and the axles. Archibald Brown was not the random victim of a German bomb – he had been targeted for murder, and the culprit was much closer to home.

The police questioned Nurse Mitchell about the events of the fatal day, and it soon transpired that all had not been as normal. When she had arrived at Summerfields that afternoon she went to the shelter to get the chair as usual, but found to her surprise that the inner door was locked. She went to the house and told Mrs Brown, who was equally mystified. As they approached the shelter they heard the bolt on the inner door slide back, and Eric emerged. Asked what he was doing he said he was looking for something. The chair was removed and prepared as usual, but neither of the women noticed anything different about it.

Superintendent Totterdell of the Essex constabulary was on leave at the time of the explosion but was soon recalled and attended a meeting at which he was directed to assume responsibility for the investigation. He questioned Mrs Brown who was unable to offer any explanation of what had occurred. No one knew the contents of her husband's will. He had been a difficult patient, and was often bad tempered but at other times he could be pleasant and considerate. Although Eric had noticed that

The remains of the bathchair on which Archibald Brown was sitting. (Essex Police Museum)

Archibald's condition had worsened and had said 'I wonder how you stick it', father and son had been on good terms. Her other son, sixteen-year-old Colin, was at college in Southend studying accountancy. He, too, had got on well with his father.

Archibald Brown was buried on Friday 30 July. Mrs Brown hesitated to question her quiet, moody son, but some three weeks later she asked him why he had been in the shelter on the day of the tragedy. He replied that he had been looking for a knife. Mrs Brown was satisfied with that explanation. To her, Eric showed no outward sign that he had the guilt of a terrible crime on his conscience.

Identifying the murder weapon was of the first importance. The fragments resembled some kind of mine, yet the normal pressure required to explode such a device was some 200 to 300lb – far more than the weight of the victim. The murder weapon was eventually identified as a Hawkins no. 75 anti-tank mine, a device which by its nature directs the main force of its blast vertically, an additional reason why Nurse Mitchell had survived. Enquiries were made, and it was found that Eric Brown had had access to just such a device.

When Eric had been in the Army he had attended instructional lectures given by a Sergeant S.F. Smith, part of whose syllabus included the assembly and ignition of mines. On 21 April 1943, the subject of Smith's lecture was the no. 75 Hawkins grenade mine. Brown had for a time been an orderly at his unit's office, and had access to stores where the mines were kept. There were 175 mines in the store of which 144 were operational. Not only that, but he had the necessary knowledge to be able to make adjustments to the mine so that a weight of only some 40 to 70lb would be enough to make it explode. The police conducted some experiments which showed that if a

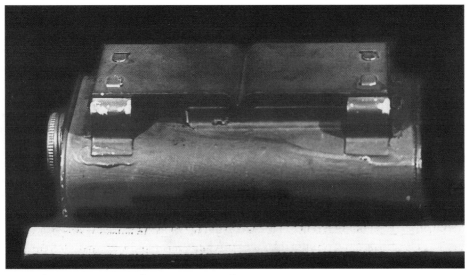

A Hawkins no. 75 anti-tank mine. (Essex Police Museum)

mine was placed under the seat of an identical chair, it would not be immediately noticeable, even to someone seated in the chair. Clearly Eric had both the means and the opportunity to commit the murder, but what was his motive?

On 20 August Eric was taken to Rayleigh Police Station where he was cautioned and asked to explain his presence in the air-raid shelter on the day of the murder. Present were Totterdell and Inspectors Draper and Barkway. Eric was uncommunicative at first, but after a time, Draper and Barkway left to get lunch, and alone with Totterdell, Eric began to open up. The superintendent, a man with thirty-one years of experience in the police force, let him talk, and when the other officers returned, Eric made and signed a voluntary statement. He was then arrested and charged with his father's murder.

The police had always felt that Mrs Brown had not revealed all she could about the relationship between father and son, but with Eric under arrest, she sought them out to tell the unhappy tale. For reasons which she could never explain, her husband had always favoured their younger son, and had taken a dislike to Eric. Long before her husband had become disabled, the boy's home life had been well-nigh unbearable from his father's constant persecution, such that she had been afraid to let them sit next to each other at mealtimes. Archibald would strike his older son for making even a slight noise, and sometimes for no reason at all. Colin would be allowed to go out and play while Eric was kept indoors writing out lines for some trivial fault. Other punishments were being locked in a dark cupboard or store-shed, and being made to run up and down the length of the hallway until distressed and exhausted. As soon as he was eleven he was sent to a boarding school in Walthamstow, a separation from the family home which can only have been a relief. He had not performed well at school, and failed his matriculation. At home once more, and working as a junior clerk in Barclays Bank, the bullying did not cease, and became so bad that Eric was obliged to take his Sunday lunch in a different room from the rest of the family. Since her husband's illness, however, it seemed that father and son had got along better, and Eric had done all he could to help the stricken man.

Her own life with Archibald had never been happy. He had forbidden her to visit her mother and she had had to do so in secret. When the family had gone out for a drive no one had been permitted to speak. A happy side effect of Archibald's declining condition had been the cessation of these miserable excursions. He had bullied her in many petty ways, and she had often thought of leaving him, even having a suitcase packed ready.

Mrs Brown said she had done all for her husband that a wife could and should do, but it seemed that however hard she tried she could do nothing right. The constant pain and frustrations of his illness had made him unmanageable and unpleasant, even cruel. He would upset the food she had given to him, and used constantly to summon her by ringing a bell, often, it seemed not out of necessity but spite. Once he had called her to say that a flower was out of position in a vase. The strain was wearing her down. It was something that Eric had been aware of as she had written to him about it while he was away, and indeed it had been terribly apparent to him during his time at home on leave.

On Monday 20 September Private Eric James Brown appeared at Southend Police Court charged with the murder of his father; Mr J.F. Claxton represented the Director of Public Prosecutions, and Mr J.P. Nolan appeared for the accused. Eric, still a month shy of his twentieth birthday, sat quiet and boyishly bespectacled, his dark hair neatly combed. The prime exhibit was the twisted remains of the wheelchair, together with a sad array of tattered cushions and blankets and Brown's pyjama jacket.

On the following day the explosives expert Captain R.G. Baker gave evidence, and stated that if the corner supports below the pressure plate on the mine were removed, and the plate was allowed to rest on the body of the mine, far less pressure than normal was required to make it explode. It was his opinion that Eric Brown had altered the mine in that manner.

As Nolan questioned Mrs Brown the full story of her husband's cruelty emerged. In the last two years she admitted, he had been physically violent towards her. When irritated, he would tip his tea over her, or grab her clothes and pull her to the ground, and on one occasion he had tried to strangle her. During the final four months of his life his attitude towards her had become increasingly unpleasant week by week.

When Inspector Barkway referred to the statement made by Eric at the police station, Nolan suddenly intervened. 'At this stage I am challenging the statement made at the opening of the case and about to be heard in detail now. According to my instructions, my client was induced to make the statement not only by a promise, but by a threat.'

Turning to the witness he asked, 'Did Detective Inspector Draper say at the interview "We know your mother is at the bottom of this somehow, and we have accumulated a lot of evidence and know more about you than you know yourself." Or words to that effect?'

'No,' said Barkway.

'Did Inspector Draper say: "We are here to help you, and if you do not tell us the truth we can make things very unpleasant for your mother, who has suffered a lot and is suffering now"?'

'No.'

'Did Inspector Draper say: "We know your mother had led a Hell of a life, and if you were any kind of a man at all you would come clean"?'

'Certainly not.'

Barkway readily agreed that Mrs Brown had been at the police station for nearly five hours, but denied that he or any other officer who had interviewed the accused had made either threats or promises to him.

Nolan's last-ditch attempt to have Eric's statement declared inadmissible had failed. The Bench ruled it could be given in evidence and it was read out in court:

I want to tell you the whole story. For this last four and a half years, and even before that, life has ceased to exist for my mother, but has become a complete drudgery as a result of my father's treatment to [sic] her. I decided that the only real way in which my mother could lead a normal life, and for my father to be released from his sufferings, was for him to die mercifully. I therefore decided to cause his death in a manner which would leave him no longer in suffering. This was only decided upon a matter of a few days before his death.

Eric's statement went on to describe how he had taken a grenade mine, with ignition and detonator as 'an act of devilment' only, and with no other intention. He had brought it home in his attaché case, and hidden it in a toolbox in the air-raid shelter.

After nearly a fortnight of seeing just exactly what my mother was forced to endure, I realised that this could not be allowed to go on. Primarily for my mother's sake, but also, to a lesser degree, for my father's sake, I placed the grenade underneath my father's chair, not realising at the time, that although it would kill him, just what his death would mean to me and all those near him. My father is now out of his suffering, and I earnestly hope that my mother will now have a much more happy and normal life. This I declare is the only motive I had for bringing about my father's death. His death was, in truth, a great shock to me, but what I did I am not afraid to answer for.

Eric Brown was committed for trial at the next Essex Assizes. Mr Nolan entered a plea of not guilty and reserved his defence.

The trial was held on 4 November at the Shire Hall, Chelmsford before Mr Justice Atkinson. The prosecution was conducted by Sir Charles Doughty KC and Mr J.C. Llewellyn, while Eric, who remained calm and unmoved throughout the proceedings, was represented by Mr (later Sir) Cecil Havers KC and Mr Wilfrid Fordham.

The public galleries were crowded with spectators, most of whom were quite unable to see the dock. One man, unable to find any seating at all, even on the most basic benches, decided to sit on the floor, much to the displeasure of the police officers in charge. He was made to get up, but his fellow spectators obligingly shuffled themselves to one side and made room for him at the end of the row.

The reporter for the *Essex Newsman and Maldon Express* was seated next to two American soldiers and before proceedings commenced, discussed with

Marks left on the road from the explosion of the mine at Rayleigh. (Essex Police Museum)

them the differences between English and American law. They took the view that it was important that the public be admitted to trials so that any injustice would be exposed. The reporter explained to them that corruption was unheard of in English courts, and in any case the press was present. 'The press!' they exclaimed, in horrified unison. 'You said the press? Why, they just print anything they're paid to print!'

The defence did not dispute that Brown had been deliberately killed by his son, but entered a plea of not guilty by reason of insanity. To be successful the defence had to prove either that Eric had not known what he was doing, or if he did then he did not know it was wrong. On the face of it, they were on shaky ground. The act of stealing a mine, concealing it, altering the mechanism and then planting it shows a high degree of organisation and premeditation, and Eric's secretive behaviour and statement show that he was well aware that he was breaking the law. Nurse Mitchell, who limped as she entered the witness box, confirmed that Brown had been violent towards his wife, who was thoroughly frightened of him. The nurse was made of sterner stuff. Asked if Brown had been violent towards her she replied, 'I told him before I went there that although it was his house, I should be the "boss" to put it plainly.' Brown, she agreed, had certainly been very exacting in his requirements of his wife. 'He tried it with me,' she said, leaving the court in no doubt that he had failed. 'I think he took advantage of his wife.'

The judge asked Nurse Mitchell about how Brown had been placed in the chair. She said she always led him to the chair and he then 'plopped' into the seat. In common with everyone else in court she could not understand how the mine had not gone off when he sat down.

Eric's mental history was now of crucial concern. Mrs Brown revealed that Eric had always been an exceptionally nervous boy, and was often moody and depressed. He had not done well at school and did not mix with the other boys. In his early days he had had a stammer. Speaking quietly to a sympathetic court, the onlookers struck by the likeness in the faces of mother and son, she said that Eric had been devoted to her. Nevertheless she felt that father and son had been on good terms in the last two years.

Detective Inspector Barkway gave evidence of enquiries he had made which indicated that there was insanity in Eric Brown's family. A grandfather, a great-grandfather and an aunt had all been mentally unstable. One of the men had hanged himself. Barkway had also made enquiries at Barclays Bank where Eric had once worked. He was told that while Eric was promising and capable, he sometimes suffered from mental lapses or brainstorms, during which he threw his hands up into the air then hammered on his desk with his fists. There had been irregularities in his dealings with some cheques, and he also admitted having misappropriated £5 10s in cash and stamps. He had no explanation for his actions, and at once returned the money. The bank, having come to the conclusion that he was mentally unbalanced, declined to prosecute and asked him to resign.

Captain Bell was Eric's commanding officer in the Army. He had perceived nothing more than a certain nervousness or self-consciousness in the young man. His character had been good, and there was nothing abnormal in his conduct. To be fair, while in the Army, Eric had been away from the undoubted stresses of his home life, and his behaviour might have been expected to show less signs of abnormality.

Neurologist and psychiatrist Dr Rowland Hill had examined Eric in Chelmsford prison on 18 October, and told the court that he had concluded the young man to be in the early stages of schizophrenia. He believed that Eric lived in a fantasy of his own, and had never become properly adjusted to the outside world. When questioned, Eric had answered in a slow halting fashion, with a tendency to break off in the middle of a sentence and go off into a daydream. Asked why he had killed his father he gave only vague answers. He had said that if someone had been standing by his side to tell him what the result of his action would be, he would never have done it, but he felt he had done God's will – he then burst into tears.

'I think,' said Hill, ignoring the evidence of Eric's tampering with the mechanism of the mine, 'he picked up the bomb in a wave of emotion – like a person in a dream – and that he put it instinctively under the cushion of the chair. I do not think he thought it out in a deliberate way.'

It was the job of Sir Charles Doughty to throw some doubt on the suggestion that Eric was not responsible for his actions. He cross-examined Hill, who declared that if the defendant had no one to take care of him or shield him, he would regard him as certifiably insane.

'Could a man who is certifiable get a good character in the Army over a period of nine months?' queried Sir Charles.

'Yes, during a lucid interval,' said Hill.

'You think a lucid interval would extend over nine months?'

'That is very common with this complaint.'

Mr Justice Atkinson had already formed an opinion of Eric Brown's mental state. 'According to his statement he knew very well what he was doing,' he observed.

Hill admitted that the accused had made a logical statement to the police, but that statement, he pointed out, had been made well after the event. He then revealed that Eric had told him he had tried to blow himself up in the shelter with the mine, but it would not go off.

Dr R.G. Lyster, the medical officer of Chelmsford Prison, was called and said he had seen and talked to Eric daily since his admission to the prison hospital on 21 August. In his opinion, Eric was sane. He had been very reserved when he first arrived, but had gradually become more communicative. There was only one indication of insanity. On 25 October Eric had tried to commit suicide by cutting his neck with a knife. It was not a serious wound, but Lyster thought the attempt was genuine. Cross-examined by Havers, Lyster said that in coming to his opinion he had taken into account both the defendant's own history and family history. Lyster did not regard Eric as perfectly normal; indeed, he thought he was not mentally stable, but that instability was not such that he could actually say that Eric was insane.

'There are many stages between perfect sanity and insanity,' observed the judge.

'Yes, my Lord.'

Recalled, Dr Hill said that the attempted suicide was highly consistent with a person suffering from schizophrenia. 'He told me that he came to prison in a happy buoyant frame of mind, and that he suddenly

Rayleigh Mill. (Author's Collection)

realised for the first time that by what he had done people might call him a murderer. That had a depressing effect on him and he attempted suicide.'

Mr Justice Atkinson, who clearly felt that Eric did not fit the strict legal definition of insanity, said in his final address to the jury, 'According to the boy's statement, he had a clear recollection of what he had done, and he gave his reasons. You have to decide whether his act was an emotional momentary impulse of which Dr Hill has spoken.'

Perhaps the jury cared little for strict legal definitions. Whether or not Eric had known what he was doing he was clearly unstable. Neither were they about to do anything to add to the sufferings of the crushed woman who had so devotedly nursed her violent husband. After three quarters of an hour, the jury returned the verdict that Eric Brown was guilty of the murder of his father, but insane.

Mr Justice Atkinson addressed Eric Brown. 'It is my duty,' he said – and only those in court would know how much the word 'duty' was emphasised – 'to order you to be kept in custody as a criminal lunatic, in such place and manner as the Court shall direct, until his Majesty's pleasure be known.'

According to local knowledge, Nurse Mitchell was able to return to nursing, although she walked with a limp and was left with a disability in one arm. Eric Brown was committed to an asylum and was released in 1975. It is not known if he is still alive.

Rayleigh Mill is no longer active, but its sails were restored in the 1970s and the handsome building now houses a museum. Its image forms the crest of the Rochford district coat of arms.

There is one thought that lingers on in the wake of this case. Eric Brown may possibly have had a personality disorder but he was neither unobservant nor unintelligent. He knew that his father was routinely placed into his chair by Mrs Brown and the nurse, and must have expected that the mine would detonate as soon as his father's weight hit the seat. If he had really killed his father for his mother's sake, why did he do so in a way that would probably kill or maim her as well?

10

LAST TAXI TO BIRCH, 1943–4

Between the villages of Messing and Birch Green there is an area of farmland crossed by some unusually straight roads. It is all that remains of Birch Airfield. The site was originally allocated to the United States 8th Air Force in August 1942 as part of the drive to establish a massive USA presence in Britain in preparation for the planned liberation of Europe. Birch was to be a heavy bomber base, with three runways, fifty hard standings, two hangars and accommodation for 2,900 personnel. In the autumn of that year, however, American air resources were diverted to North Africa, and as a result the plan to establish bases in the UK was postponed until the summer of 1943. Construction work on the new airfield was eventually carried out by the men of the 846th Engineer Battalion of the US Army.

By October 1943 the runways had been completed and the hard standings were just commencing construction, but even before it was brought into use, there were signs that it was becoming obsolete. The 8th Air Force had found they no longer required it, and it was transferred to the 9th, who eventually decided that they didn't need it either.

Many of the men working on the airbase were African-American, at a time when most British residents had never seen a black person except in films. Individually, there were Britons whose outward acceptance masked distrust and fear, but most were welcoming. They deplored the white Americans' insistence on imposing a colour-bar, and found the African-American soldiers friendlier and better mannered. There was also a more natural sympathy with people who, like families in wartime Britain were unused to luxuries, a lack which the white soldiers frequently complained about. The black troops, used to rigid racial demarcation at home, found a freedom of movement and relationships they had never before experienced. With money to spend, and all temptations easily satisfied, it was not surprising that the men, while working hard, played still harder. City life was a short train ride away, and local taxis were available at all hours.

Harry Claude Hailstone, a Colchester cab-driver, was twenty-eight years old. He suffered from a deformity of his hands, which was due to an accident some years previously, but this did not prevent him from driving a car or taking up his original profession of ladies' hairdresser. One foot was also affected, and he walked with a limp. Harry's father, H.E. Hailstone, had done twenty-seven years of service in the Army, and wore South African and First

World War medals. As a private in the Boer War he had once volunteered to lead the brigade through the encircling enemy, thus earning himself the distinction of being the only private ever to have led a general. The Hailstones had five children, a son who had died some years before, Harry, Roy William who was in the RAF, 18-year-old Joan who belonged to the Women's Land Army and Mrs Vera Wheeler who worked for the Ordnance.

In August 1940 the Hailstones were residing at East Hill, Colchester, when a bomb fell at the back of the house. Mrs Gertrude Hailstone received a head injury and never fully recovered. She died twelve months later, aged fifty-seven. The Hailstones moved to 30 Maidenburgh Street, Colchester, and Harry was obliged to give up hairdressing. He worked for Davey Paxman and Co., an engineering company, but in July 1943

Harry Claude Hailstone. (Essex Police Museum)

turned to taxi driving, and was employed by Blackwell's taxi cab service. Everything known about him, which, admittedly was said after his death, suggests that he was a likeable, easygoing, popular and law-abiding man.

In April 1942 tragedy again hit the Hailstone family when Roy William was reported killed in action in the Middle East.

In September 1943 Harry took lodgings at 127 Maldon Road, the home of Sidney Charles Pearce, a shipwright, and his wife, Mary Ellen, and changed his employer to William Bucknell of Parsons Heath Garage, Harwich Road.

Shortly after 11 p.m. on the night of Tuesday 7 December 1943, Harry Hailstone called in at his lodgings to tell Mrs Pearce he was not coming home for supper. He had two fares in his taxi who he was taking to Birch.

Knowing that this must mean the airfield she asked, 'Who have you got in the car? Have you got two white officers?' (When later asked why she had wanted to know this she said, 'Because drivers don't like taking coloured men. I was hoping he had white Americans.')

'No, two niggers,' he replied. 'One is a Lieutenant and the other is a Private'. Hailstone then left, saying he would be back in half an hour, and she heard the car drive away. She waited up for him until 1 a.m. but he never returned. She did not suspect that anything was wrong, assuming that either he had picked up an unexpected fare, or had run out of petrol and decided to sleep in the cab. On the Wednesday she went out for the day and did not expect to see her lodger again until Thursday. She never, therefore, reported him missing.

That evening, Hailstone's abandoned taxi was found by a police constable in Haynes Green Lane just off the Maldon road. In the car were found a

Haynes Green Lane, where the taxi was abandoned. (Author's Collection)

man's jacket and a mackintosh with a bloodstained collar. The sleeves of the jacket were inside out, as if the garment had been pulled off the wearer from behind. Superintendent Totterdell was at once advised of the discovery, and he went to Copford police station where the clothing had been taken. Finding Harry Hailstone's driving licence, he interviewed Mrs Pearce, and confirmed that the clothing and the cab both belonged to the missing man. Usefully, she was able to give the police details of what possessions Hailstone might have had on him.

Totterdell and Inspector Draper now went to examine the cab. There was a small amount of external damage, but no sign that it had been involved in a serious accident. It seemed to have stopped in the usual way – but on the right side of the road. This and Mrs Pearce's evidence suggested strongly to the police that the last person to drive the car was an American. A fierce struggle had obviously taken place inside the cab. Scattered on the floor were papers belonging to Hailstone, his empty wallet, and gloves. The upholstery was damaged and the telephone flex and parcel net had been dragged from their moorings. Unsurprisingly, there were spots of blood in the car, one of which was on the rear seat.

Totterdell felt sure that Hailstone had been attacked from behind. Despite his disability the driver was a young, vigorous man, weighing between 11 and 12 stone. He would have put up a good fight. It looked as though after he had been overcome, his body must have been lifted onto the back seat, and his assailant then drove the car to where it was found.

But where was Harry Hailstone? By now it must have been clear to the police that they were looking for a corpse. They began by making a thorough search of the area around the cab, and when this yielded nothing, widened the radius, concentrating on the road leading to the nearby American Army camps. Officers and men of the local garrisons came to assist the police in their search. The only thing that turned up was another mackintosh, which was found 6 miles east of where the cab had been left, and had bloodstains down its front. Although it was not of military style, it was of Canadian manufacture and had an American Service emblem on one of the pockets. It was also labelled with the owner's name – Captain J.J. Weber.

Enquiries revealed that while Captain Weber was stationed at the Canadian General Hospital in Cuckfeld, Sussex, on 5 December he had been taking a course at the 18th Canadian General Hospital, Cherry Tree Camp, Colchester, only a short distance from Birch Airfield. Soon Weber was being interviewed by Sussex CID. Weber said that on the night of 5 December he had been at Liverpool Street station in London, to get a train back to Colchester when he had met a black American army sergeant. They had struck up an acquaintance and travelled together. At Colchester he had invited the man back to his room where there was a bottle of whisky. Weber had been absent from the room for a short while, leaving his new acquaintance there. On his return he found that the sergeant had left, taking with him the bottle of whisky, and his mackintosh. Weber identified the bloodstained coat found in the ditch as his. Its pockets had been emptied, and he was missing £5 in cash, a torch, a pair of gloves and a Rolex watch.

The police were confident that the widening search would eventually be successful, and on 9 December, the body of Harry Hailstone was found. To the east of the airfield on the Maldon road was Birch Rectory, its grounds bordered at the roadside by a steep bank and hedge topped with two strands of barbed wire. Constable Edgar Snowling had been making a search of hedgerows and ditches when he saw something lying on the inside bank about 6ft from the roadway in the Rectory garden. It was not immediately visible from the road, but from the top of the bank Snowling saw it was a man's body lying twisted in the brambles as if he had been roughly thrown over the hedge and had tumbled down there. He was fully clothed apart from his hat, jacket and overcoat, and his face was covered with blood.

Totterdell was at once alerted and went to the spot. Hailstone's landlord, Sidney Pearce, was brought there to identify the body. It was the missing taxi-driver.

Totterdell believed that the murder had taken place in the taxi, then the body had been driven to the bank, lifted out, and pushed under the strands of barbed wire – there was blood on the lower one – and sent rolling down the slope. The weight of the body suggested that two men had been involved. Since it was later shown that Hailstone must have been killed on the night he went missing, suspicion naturally fell on the two black soldiers in his cab.

After being viewed by Essex County pathologist Dr Francis Camps, the body was removed in an ambulance and taken to Colchester Mortuary for the post mortem. He found bruises on the head, the result of repeated heavy blows, probably from a fist. The nose and lips were swollen to two or three times their normal size, and there were fingernail marks on the neck. He noted the deformity of the hands which would have reduced the young man's ability to defend himself. Camps had no doubt in giving the cause of death as asphyxia caused by manual strangulation.

With the case now undoubtedly one of murder, Weber had some explaining to do, but fortunately, an orderly recalled his returning on the night of 5 December with the black sergeant, who, while running off with the whisky and coat, had managed to forget his gas mask. Inside the case were a serial number and a name – J. Hill.

It was not hard to find J. Hill – he was stationed at Birch, and was one of the Engineer Regiment engaged in the construction of the site. He admitted that the mask was his, but it had not been in his possession on 5 December. Four days earlier he had lent it to another member of the regiment, Private George E. Fowler.

Fowler, of company E, 356th Engineer General Service Regiment, was twenty-two years old. He had attended high school, but had not graduated, leaving in 1939, obliged to go to work because of his mother's illness. In 1942, at Peoria, Illinois, he had entered the army as a cook, but had later transferred to the Engineers. He had only one previous conviction, for being absent without leave.

The site where Harry Hailstone's body was dumped. (Essex Police Museum)

When questioned, Fowler, who did not then know the police had the gas mask, agreed that he had borrowed it from Hill before he went to London on leave, but claimed he had left it at the Liberty Club in Euston Square where he had been staying. Fowler had spent his leave in the time-honoured fashion, which involved women and alcohol, and said he had no recollection of how he had got back to camp. He did not mention meeting Weber on 5 December and claimed to have been in London all week, returning on the evening of 8 December, the day after the murder. Somewhere during the week-long pub crawl, he had acquired a Sergeant's blouse, but had no idea how or from whom.

Detaining Fowler, Totterdell arranged for a search of his quarters. He found a Sergeant's blouse, which had traces of blood on it, and a pawn ticket for a Rolex watch. Shown the ticket, Fowler declared that he had never pawned anything in his life. He then supplied another story in which the gas mask had been taken from the Liberty Club by someone else. He still maintained that he was in London on the night of the murder. The watch was recovered from the pawnshop and later identified by Weber as the one stolen from his quarters. Totterdell arranged for Fowler to be locked in a cell at Colchester police station. While there, Fowler tried unsuccessfully to hide Weber's torch by making a small hole in the window and pushing it through, but it was held in place by the blackout board and retrieved by an observant constable.

The pawn ticket furnished another valuable clue, for it was in an envelope on the back of which was written a name – Charlie Huntley. Huntley, of Company B, was happy to tell Totterdell about having been at the West Indies club in London on 6 December when he had met a soldier called George. It was obvious from his description of events that George was Private George Fowler. Fowler had asked him to pawn a Rolex watch for him. The ticket had been handed back to him in an envelope on which Huntley had written his name before passing it to George.

There was now a firm link between the man in custody and the bloodstained coat found on the Maldon road, but it was obvious to the police that a second man was involved. Huntley had mentioned that George had been with another soldier called Private Leatherberry.

When Fowler was questioned again, the mounting evidence that he was involved in a serious crime was enough to elicit a quite different tale from the one he had first told. He now admitted meeting up with Weber in the buffet bar at Liverpool Street station on 5 December. After a few drinks they had caught the train to Colchester and then went by cab to the Cherry Tree Camp. The drinking continued, but when Fowler wanted to return to his own quarters, Weber told him he had already called a cab for him. The cab did not arrive, and Weber had then suggested that Fowler stay the night and offered to make up a bed for him in his room. Quite what Fowler made of this friendly offer he did not say, but he left, he claimed, at 6.15 p.m. after accepting the coat as a gift.

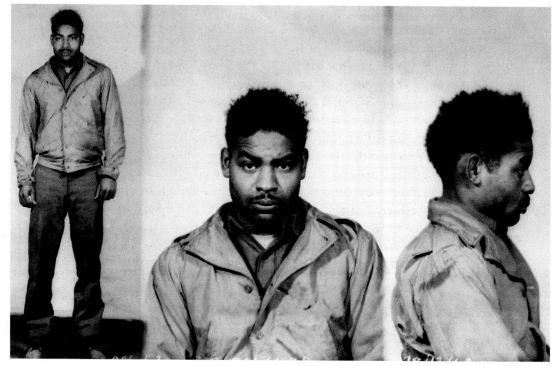

George E. Fowler. (Essex Police Museum)

Fowler had left Cherry Tree Camp, boarding a bus on which, coincidentally, were a number of friends. The intention to return to camp was somehow forgotten, and became instead a visit to the White Horse public house. Private Leatherberry had suggested they go back to London. Fowler was reluctant as he had already been away for two days longer than permitted by his pass, an offence for which he was ultimately disciplined. Nevertheless, he allowed himself to be persuaded by Leatherberry to return to London.

The trip to London seemed to involve more drinking. Fowler had met up with Leatherberry again on the evening of 7 December which was when, he said, he had found the envelope with the pawn ticket in it. The two men returned to Colchester that night, and on the way, Leatherberry suggested to Fowler that they should hire a taxi to take them to camp and rob the driver on the way. Fowler didn't say whether he believed his companion or not, but the two men continued the journey together. It was cold, and Leatherberry had been complaining of the chill, so he had given him the mackintosh he had got from Weber, and Leatherberry wore it for the rest of the evening.

They were back in Colchester at 10.45 p.m. and took a cab. Fowler remembered the driver stopping off briefly at his lodgings, and Leatherberry told him the driver had gone to get a gun. Four miles further on, Fowler had wanted to relieve himself, and so the taxi stopped while he got out. Thus occupied, he heard Leatherberry calling to him, and when he got back to the cab found Leatherberry standing up in the back of the cab holding the driver with his left hand and punching him with his right. He shouted to Fowler to help him, saying, claimed Fowler in his statement, that 'I was just as much in it as he was'.

By the time Fowler got back in the cab the driver had gone limp, and Leatherberry was dragging him onto the back seat. 'He's out,' he said, and Fowler assumed that the man was simply unconscious. 'We've got to stick together,' he went on, rifling through the driver's pockets.

Leatherberry now said that Fowler had to help him get rid of the body. Fowler took the feet and Leatherberry the head, and they carried the man across the road and pushed the body under a wire fence. Fowler had wanted to return to camp, but Leatherberry insisted on driving to Maldon to try and get a train to London, but once there, they found the last train had gone. Fowler then took over the wheel and drove back to camp, abandoning the taxi. Fowler said he had slept in a hut, and had no idea what had happened to either Leatherberry or the coat after that. A private of the Engineers had seen the cab in a lane near the air base at about midnight, and a man in a raincoat had been making a telephone call from a nearby kiosk, but Fowler denied that this was him.

Totterdell next proceeded to interview Private J.C. Leatherberry of Company A, 356th Engineer Service Regiment. Leatherberry, who came from Crystal Springs, Mississippi, was twenty-one years of age, and like Fowler,

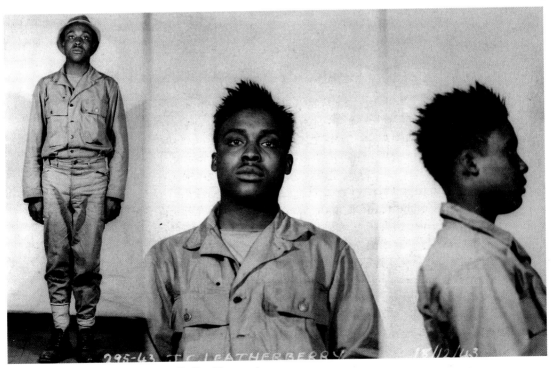

J.C. Leatherberry. (Essex Police Museum)

had only one previous conviction for being absent without leave. He admitted meeting up with Fowler in the White Horse, and the drunken jaunt to London, but said, as Fowler had initially, that he was in London on the night of the murder. In Leatherberry's hut the police found bloodstained clothing, and he was arrested and locked in Colchester police station. Scrapings were taken from underneath the fingernails of both men. Blue fibres were found in both sets of scrapings, similar to the fabric of the dead man's clothing. There was a trace of blood under one of Fowler's nails, but blood under all of Leatherberry's, none of it sufficient for grouping. Hailstone, unlike the two soldiers, was of the relatively rare AB blood group, and this matched dried blood found on Weber's raincoat and on Leatherberry's clothing.

Neither of the men was in possession of much money when arrested, but Hailstone, it was estimated, would have had not much more than £12 on him when he was killed.

The inquest opened at St Albright's Hospital, Stanway, on Monday 13 December before Mr Reginald Proudfoot, the deputy coroner for North East Essex. It took place in the tiny Master's Room, which required the attendees to climb a narrow flight of stone steps. 'We shall not go into details for reasons which you shall hear and understand,' said Proudfoot, as the black-clad girl clerk seated to his right took notes in longhand. 'I only propose to take formal evidence of identification and medical evidence as to the cause of death, and then adjourn while enquiries are proceeding. Whether you will ever be troubled again is very doubtful. I hope not.' After the completion of the evidence the inquest was adjourned for four weeks.

On 14 December Leatherberry was questioned at length, but adamant that he had told the truth, said he had nothing more to add to his statement. He appeared in two identification parades that day. In one, Fowler picked him out as the man he had accompanied on the night of the murder, and the owners of the premises where he stated he had stayed the night in London identified him as the man who had been there on 6 December but not on the following night.

Both Leatherberry and Fowler were charged with murder and handed over to the American military authorities. They left Colchester police station accompanied by armed US military police, and were driven away.

As they awaited trial, Christmas approached and the newspapers provided another side of the coin of the relationship between American troops and British residents. The *Essex Chronicle* reviewed a booklet written by 'Yankee soldiers' called *Hallo America* which was designed to keep Britons informed about American customs, and especially to tell them about the realities of life in the USA as distinct from what was popularly depicted in the cinema. It also reported that American 'coloured troops' had given up their rations in order to provide a party for 400 local children. The partygoers were taken by bus to a location not revealed in the article, presumably a US Army base, where they were entertained by a film show, given brightly wrapped presents, and treated

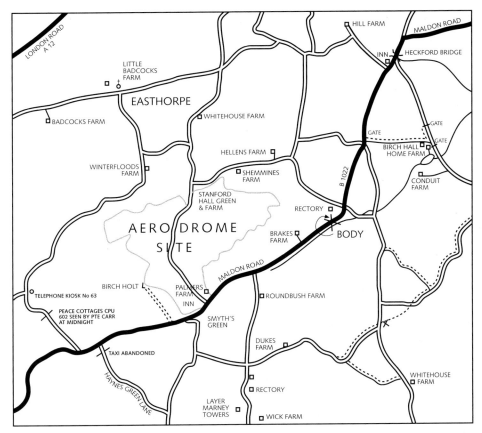

The area of Birch airfield in 1943.

to a slap-up tea. The happy children were then driven home. The article was headed 'The Darkies give a party', which would be thought unthinkable today, but the warm appreciation of the gesture was obvious.

In a unique arrangement, the two courts-martial of Leatherberry and Fowler were carried on independently and simultaneously in different rooms of the same building, Ipswich Town Hall, commencing on Wednesday 19 January. The trial of Leatherberry was presided over by Lieutenant Colonel Zeigler, and nine other officers were present, two of whom were African-American. Fowler was the principal witness for the prosecution. Questioned by Captain Daniel Pinsky, he said that he was outside the cab when he heard a bumping noise, and Leatherberry said 'Aren't you going to help me?'. By the time he got back to the cab the driver was already half way over the front seat into the back. Leatherberry had taken hold of the driver's throat with one hand and was pounding him with the other. At this point it was decided to allow Fowler to demonstrate in court what he had seen. Captain Albert Anderson, his defence lawyer, volunteered to act as victim, and seated in a chair, Fowler came up behind him, placed his left hand on the officer's throat, lifted him half way over the back of the chair and swung his fist towards the man's face. Fowler added that he saw Leatherberry going through the driver's pockets. It had, he said, been Leatherberry's suggestion to rob the taxi driver.

'Did you say "No, don't do it"?' asked Lieutenant C.E. Crane, defending Leatherberry.

'I did not say anything about it,' replied Fowler, 'I thought he was just kidding.'

One of the African-American officers asked, 'Do you fully understand that you are as much involved as Leatherberry because you were with him?'

'I did not know that,' said Fowler. 'I do not see why I should be.'

Once Fowler had given his evidence he crossed to the second court where his own trial commenced. He was charged with murder, as well as the minor offences of stealing a raincoat, a watch and £5 from Captain Weber, and pleaded not guilty. His evidence was the same as in the earlier court.

'I did not think he was dead,' he said of Hailstone. 'I did not think a person could be so easily killed. I would not have any idea in my mind to do a thing like this. Back home I have nice parents.'

At 9.30 p.m. Leatherberry's court-martial was adjourned to the following Monday to allow his counsel to obtain more evidence. He now crossed to the second court to give evidence against Fowler. At first he was unwilling, saying he knew nothing about Fowler, but at last he was persuaded, his counsel sitting beside him to give advice. Leatherberry stated that he had spent some time with Fowler on 6 December but denied being in the taxi at all. Captain David Harman, prosecuting, maintained that in this 'murder of the most cold-blooded type' Fowler and Leatherberry had been equally involved. Captain Anderson, defending, pointed out that Fowler had only helped move the body, and had not taken part in either the murder or the robbery. His client had, he admitted, displayed a lack of acumen in not taking Leatherberry's intentions seriously.

The court at Fowler's trial sat for 12 hours, the proceedings ending at 1.30 a.m. Fowler was found guilty of murder, but the court, impressed by the clear and straightforward way in which he had given his evidence, was inclined to be lenient. He was told that he would be dishonourably discharged and sentenced to life imprisonment with hard labour, to be served at the United States Penitentiary Lewisburg, Pennsylvania.

On 24 January, Leatherberry entered the witness box, and stated that he had nothing to do with the murder of Harry Hailstone. He suggested that the blood on his hands and clothes originated from a fight, but Hailstone's rare blood group was a telling factor, and Leatherberry was obliged to admit that he had changed his account of where in London he was supposed to have stayed on the night of the murder. Two witnesses were brought for the defence, the manageress of a London café who stated that he had been there on the night of 7 December with a girl, and was there again the next morning, and a married shorthand typist called Jean who said she had spent the night of 7 December with him.

Some of the type AB blood had been on Leatherberry's underwear, the inference being that this was transferred from his hands when he next urinated after the murder. His claim that the traces were due to intercourse failed, as Jean's blood group was A.

Fowler, now in blue overalls, was recalled. 'Did in fact Leatherberry strangle that taxi driver?' asked Pinsky, dramatically.

'Yes sir,' replied Fowler.

The trial ended at 11 p.m. after lasting more than fourteen hours. Lieutenant Crane told the jury that Leatherberry should be given the benefit of the doubt. The only evidence against him was Fowler's and this was necessarily biased. There were also two witnesses to show that his client had been in London on the night of the murder. In the end, however, it was the blood evidence that must have swayed the jury. Leatherberry was found guilty and sentenced to death.

The death penalty on Leatherberry was reviewed by President Eisenhower and an announcement was eventually made that sentence was to be carried out on 16 May.

In wartime Britain, part of the seventeenth-century gaol in Shepton Mallet, Somerset, was used as a military prison by the American forces. Leatherberry would have occupied a cell next to the execution chamber for three or four days prior to the appointed day. According to American custom, executions were carried out at 1 a.m. Condemned men were dressed in a regulation uniform from which any insignia or evidence of which unit they had belonged had been removed. An unusual staff perk of these American wartime executions was the food and drink provided. 'We were eating badly in this county at that time,' said Albert Pierrepoint, 'but at an American execution you could be sure of the best running buffet and unlimited canned beer.'

Pierrepoint was assisting his uncle Thomas at the execution of Leatherberry, which took place before eight personnel and twelve witnesses. Totterdell had been invited to attend but declined. The men assembled in the execution chamber at 12.52 a.m., and three minutes later the prison guards brought Leatherberry, accompanied by the Commandant of the prison, and the chaplain. One aspect of these military executions which Pierrepoint found 'sickening' was the interval of time between pinioning the prisoner and operating the drop. Pierrepoint had got the waiting time down to a maximum of twenty seconds, and it was often much less. Leatherberry, having been placed on the gallows platform, was obliged to remain there for several minutes while the charges and sentence were read out to him, the assembled company standing to attention. Despite this, he seems to have retained his composure. Asked if he had anything to say, he simply said, 'I have no statement to make, sir. I want to thank the guys for everything as they were so nice to me, the guards and everything.' In the hope of a last-minute confession, Chaplain O'Brien said, 'Do you have any statement to make to me as chaplain.' 'Sir, I want to thank you for being so nice to me and

The abandoned airfield at Birch. (Author's Collection)

for everything you have done for me,' was the frustrating response. Leatherberry maintained his wall of silence to the end, although it is safe to assume that an innocent man would have had something to say on the subject.

In the United States hanging would have been carried out with a standard length rope and an old-fashioned hangman's coiled noose. This method was not permitted in Britain, so the executioners prepared Leatherberry with a British noose, the rope running freely through a metal loop, and a drop already calculated according to his weight and build to snap his neck instantly. On a silent signal from the Commandant the platform fell at precisely 1 a.m. Private Leatherberry was officially pronounced dead eighteen minutes later.

The bodies of American servicemen executed at Shepton Mallet were buried at Brookwood cemetery in Surrey, and no identifying insignia were permitted on their burial clothes. After the war, the remains were sent to a cemetery in France where a section had been set aside for burials of 'dishonoured' individuals.

By 1946, Fowler had been transferred to the penitentiary in Atlanta, Georgia, his sentence reduced to twenty-five years. In 1950 his sentence was further reduced to twenty years and in 1960 he was released.

Birch airfield was completed in the spring of 1944, at a final cost of some £1 million*, by which time it had reverted back to the 8th Air Force, but neither the USAAF nor the RAF now had a need for it. It was used by some RAF transport squadrons early in 1945, and shortly after the end of the war, it closed down. Nowadays the area has a desolate windswept feel. Occasionally, stolen cars are abandoned there by joy riders, and the solitude may have an appeal for courting couples. Learner drivers also find it has much to recommend it. The roads, after all, are unusually straight.

* See Graham Smith's *Essex Airfields in the Second World War*, Newbury, Countryside Books, 1996.

BIBLIOGRAPHY & ACKNOWLEDGEMENTS

Chapter 1. Colchester Jack, 1744–6

Anon, *The Life and Behaviour of John Skinner*, London, J. Thompson, 1746(?)

Benham, Hervey, *The Smugglers Century: The Story of Smuggling on the Essex Coast, 1730–1830*, Chelmsford, Essex Record Office, 1986

Phillipson, David, *Smuggling, a History*, Newton Abbot, David and Charles, 1973

Wivenhoe WEA, under the tutorship of A.F.J. Brown, *Smuggling and Wivenhoe*, Colchester, Manor Press, undated

Brightlingsea parish records, Essex County Archives

Chapter 2. One Night in Walthamstow, 1751–2

Anon, *The Newgate Calendar or Malefactors Bloody Register*, London, T. Werner Laurie, 1932, pp. 518–24

Anon, *The Whole Tryal of John Swann and Elizabeth Jeffryes*, London, M. Cooper, 1752

Anon, *The Authentick Tryals of John Swan and Elizabeth Jeffryes for the murder of Mr Joseph Jeffryes of Walthamstow in Essex*, London, R. Walker, 1752

Anon, *The Authentick Memoirs of the Wicked Life and Transactions of Elizabeth Jeffryes, Spinster*, London, T. Bailey, 1752

Court Register for the Manor of Walthamstow Toney and High Hall, May 1732–May 1765. Manuscript number W35.21/2 pp. 342–3

General Advertiser

Burial records, parish of Walthamstow

International Genealogical Index

Rate books Walthamstow 1739–1751

Chapter 3. The Dagenham Outrage, 1846–58

Barking and Dagenham Post
Barking and Dagenham Recorder
Barking and Dagenham Yellow Advertiser
Essex Herald
Essex Standard
The Job
The Times

Family Record Centre, London

Chapter 4. The Clavering Poisoner, 1845–51

Essex Herald
Ludgate, E.M., *Clavering and Langley 1783–1983*, Clavering, E.M. Ludgate, 1984
The Times
Who Was Who

Files of the Essex Police Museum

Chapter 5. Sweet Lass of Buckhurst Hill, 1867–8

Essex Herald
Essex Telegraph
Evening Standard
Illustrated Police News
Johnson, C., *Victorian Buckhurst Hill – A Miscellany*, Epping, Epping Forest District Council, 1980
Telegraph
The Times

Family Record Centre, London

Chapter 6. The Man at Witham Station, 1893–1901

Colchester Gazette
Essex County Standard
Essex Telegraph
Police Gazette
The Times

Family Record Centre, London

Chapter 7. Tragedy at Southend, 1922

Evening Standard
Southend Pictorial Telegraph
Southend-on-Sea Observer
Southend Standard

Family Record Centre, London

Chapter 8. The Beast of Hornchurch, 1939

Benton, Tony, The Changing Face of Hornchurch, Stroud, Sutton, 1999
Hornchurch Council, Hornchurch Official Guide, Cheltenham and London, J. Burrow and Co. Ltd, 1939
Totterdell, G.H., Country Copper, London, George G. Harrap, 1956
The News (Hornchurch and Upminster News)
The Times
Who Was Who

Chapter 9. Explosion at Rayleigh, 1943

Essex Chronicle
Essex Newsman and Maldon Express

Feather, Fred, The Rayleigh Bath-chair Murder, History Notebook number 35, Essex, Essex Police Museum, undated
Southend-on-Sea and County Pictorial
Southend-on-Sea Observer
Southend Standard
Southend Times and Recorder
Rayleigh Urban District Council, Rayleigh Urban District Official Guide, Rayleigh, Rayleigh Urban District Council, 1961
Totterdell, G.H., Country Copper, London, George G. Harrap, 1956

Family Record Centre, London

Chapter 10. Last Taxi to Birch, 1943–4

Colchester Gazette
Disney, Francis J., Shepton Mallet Prison, Shepton Mallet, Whitstone, 1993
Essex Chronicle
Essex Newsman Herald
Evening Star
Pierrepoint, Albert, Executioner: Pierrepoint, Coronet, Sevenoaks, 1974
Record of the court martial cases of United States v. Private J.C. Leatherberry (CM 305769) and Private George E. Fowler (CM 268994), US Army Judiciary.
Smith, Graham, When Jim Crow Met John Bull: Black American Soldiers in World War II Britain, London, Tauris, 1987
——, Essex Airfields in the Second World War, Newbury, Countryside Books, 1996
Totterdell, G.H., Country Copper, London, George G. Harrap, 1956

Family Record Centre, London

I am particularly indebted to Jo Parker of the Vestry House Museum in Walthamstow, the British Library, the Newspaper Library at Colindale, Sarah Ward of the Essex Police Museum, Simon Donoghue of Havering Library Service, Linda Rhodes of the London Borough of Barking and Dagenham Local Studies Library, Mary Dennis and Linda Erickson of the US Army Judiciary. Also to my husband Gary, who has by now become used to the fact that most of our holidays and excursions seem to involve visiting a murder site.

INDEX